MW00629933

ETERNAL JOY

A Guide To Shidduchim & Marriage

ETERNAL JOY

A Guide To Shidduchim & Marriage

- MARRIED LIFE AND SHALOM BAYIS -

BASED ON THE TEACHINGS OF
THE LUBAVITCHER REBBE
RABBI MENACHEM M. SCHNEERSON

by
Rabbi Sholom B. Wineberg

**VOLUME III —
MARRIED LIFE & SHALOM BAYIS**

Published by
SICHOS IN ENGLISH
788 Eastern Parkway
Brooklyn, New York 11213
(718) 778-5436

Eternal Joy

Published and Copyrighted © by
Sichos In English
788 Eastern Parkway • Brooklyn, N.Y. 11213
Tel. (718) 778-5436

All rights reserved. No part of this publication may be reproduced in any form or by any means, including photo-copying, without permission in writing from the copyright holder or the publisher.

ISBN 1-8814-0059-X

5761 • 2001

CREDITS

Rochel Chana Schilder for editing.
Yosef Yitzchok Turner for designing the layout and typography.
Rabbi Yonah Avtzon for preparing text for publication.
Avrohom Weg for designing the cover.

TABLE OF CONTENTS

SHALOM BAYIS

ב"ה

FOREWORD

With heartfelt gratitude to G-d, we hereby present the third and concluding volume of *Eternal Joy, a Guide to Shidduchim & Marriage*, based on the Rebbe's teachings.

The present volume encompasses the Rebbe's directives and advice concerning matters that are relevant to married life — with emphasis on those matters that ensue during the first year of marriage — and *Shalom Bayis:* peace and harmony in the relationship between husband and wife.

The Rebbe has spoken about the issues of marriage and *Shalom Bayis* in many *farbrengens* (public gatherings), and has responded to the questions asked of him by numerous individuals in his *Igros Kodesh*, as well as in personal responses during *Yechidus* (personal audiences) and through his secretariat.

By studying these sources, it is possible to appreciate some of the fundamental elements of the Rebbe's approach to married life and *Shalom Bayis*.

As we have done in the first two volumes, in this volume as well we have collected[1] and translated selections from a variety of

---

1. The majority of the material in this collection has been culled from the following works: *Shidduchin V'Nisuin — Likkutei Horaois, Minhagim, U'Biurim* (Kehot, Brooklyn, 5752); *Shaarei Halachah U'Minhag* (Kehot, Kfar Chabad, 5753); *Sefer HaShlichus* (Kehot, Kfar Chabad, 5747); *Leman Tatzliach* (Eishel, Kfar Chabad, 5758); *Refuah Shleimah* (*Or Yaakov*, Kfar Chabad, 5752).

   A reader fluent in Hebrew would do well to also consult these sources. The latter three sources in particular contain much material from the Rebbe on the subjects of *shlichus*, earning a livelihood, and matters relating to conception and pregnancy.

   We have also collected considerable additional material. For the most part, this has been gathered from *Likkutei Sichos* and *Igros Kodesh*, and the various the Rebbe's letters, *sichos*, and personal responses regarding married life and *Shalom Bayis*.

It is worth reiterating the caveat stated in each of the Forewords to the first two volumes of this collection:

Firstly, the collection and the translation are our own; it is not a guide to marriage and *Shalom Bayis* authored or edited by the Rebbe.

Secondly, it is not all-encompassing. There certainly is considerably more material from the Rebbe regarding married life and *Shalom Bayis* than has been collected here.

And finally, while the Rebbe's public directives pertain to all, it is entirely possible that the personal advice the Rebbe gave one individual may not be appropriate for another. Moreover, some of the responses to individuals are not necessarily the Rebbe's final word on the matter.

What we have done to try to resolve this latter difficulty is to quote a variety of letters and *sichos*, even though some may appear different from others. The dates or sources cited may be of benefit in discerning the Rebbe's later responses. So, too, by noting that numerous answers are in the same vein, we have an indication of the Rebbe's general approach to a specific issue or matter.

Nevertheless, it must be borne in mind that the Rebbe's answer to one individual does not necessarily apply *at all* to another, as the Rebbe has pointed out on a number of occasions. To quote but two:

> "I have already expressed — and have done so *numerous* times: My answer to one individual does not

---

collections of the Rebbe's English letters, as well as from the *Kfar Chabad* and *Beis Moshiach* magazines and various "*teshuros*" issued as wedding mementos.

constitute a directive — it doesn't even constitute a response — to a second individual.[2]

On another occasion the Rebbe writes:

"It is *patently obvious* that a directive to an *individual* does not serve *at all* as a directive to the multitude, even when the issues are the same. This is particularly so when this is written as a *private* letter *to him.*

"For *most often* this depends on the conditions of the life of that individual, his personality and temperament, the possibilities that exist for him concerning that which he wrote [to me about] in his letter, *and more, and more* [reasons, not enumerated here]." [3]

In instances of doubt, etc., one would therefore do well to remember the Rebbe's exhortations to "ask one's *mashpia* or *rav*" and "seek the counsel of wise and discerning good friends."

May the marriages that are currently taking place herald and hasten the coming of the ultimate marriage celebration, the marriage and supreme union of G-d and the Jewish people.

As the Rebbe states: "The marriage of every couple ... is connected to the ultimate marriage between G-d and the Jewish people that will be consummated in the Era of Redemption."[4]

And at that time, "We will again meet with the Rebbe on this earthly plane, and he shall redeem us."[5]

To conclude on a personal note:

This *Sefer* is dedicated to my very dear friend and long-time Torah study partner, Mr. Neil N. Sosland, and his esteemed wife

---

2. Printed in *Kfar Chabad* Magazine (together with a facsimile of the Rebbe's holy handwritten response), Issue 817.
3. Printed in *Beis Moshiach* Magazine (together with a facsimile of the Rebbe's holy handwritten response), Issue 173.
4. *Sefer HaSichos 5751*, Vol. II, p. 807
5. The conclusion of *Maamar Basi LeGani*, 5711.

Blanche. Their beautiful marriage is a sterling example of true *Shalom Bayis*.

May G-d continue to grant them much *nachas* from all their wonderful children and grandchildren, and many, many more happy and healthy years together.

Sholom B. Wineberg
Overland Park, Kansas

Chof-Ches Shvat, 5761

Married
Life

Chapter One

Sustaining the Spirituality of Marriage

Marriage as an Eternal Edifice Is Attained Specifically Through Attachment To the Moshe of the Generation

In one of the *maamarim*[1] that my father-in-law, the Rebbe, presented to be learned on the second of Nissan, the day of his father's passing, he [i.e., the Rebbe] explains the verse (at the beginning of our Torah portion), "And you (Moshe) shall command the children of Israel and they shall bring you pure olive oil ... to keep a constant lamp burning."

[The Rebbe asks:] "On the face of it, it is extremely difficult to understand how it is possible for light — an entity that is but an illumination [of its source] — to contain within it the constancy [of burning without cessation], something that relates only to [its source,] the luminary."

He explains that this is the novelty of "And you [Moshe] shall command," that Moshe possesses the capacity to command and connect all Jews (with G-d) ... at which time there is revealed even within a lamp — a mere illumination — the essential power [of the luminary]. Consequently, the illumination as well is constantly attached to the eternality of the *Ein Sof*.

The Rebbe concludes that "the assistance in achieving this matter [of a degree of permanence and eternality] is through

1. Discourse titled *Zos Toras HaBayis* 5689 (*Sefer HaMaamarim Kuntreisim*, Vol. I, p. 39ff. Also printed in *Sefer HaMaamarim* 5689, p. 162ff.)

one's connection and bond (*hiskashrus*) with the rank of Moshe, the heads and leaders of the Jewish people [of each generation], the "extension of Moshe."

The above is critical as well with regard to building a house in Israel, an "eternal edifice."

... The ability for a particular house in Israel to contain the [limitless] aspect of immutability, which is the quality of an "eternal edifice," results from Moshe.

Thus, the assistance in obtaining this matter is through connecting and bonding (*hiskashrus*) with Moshe, i.e., the "extension of Moshe in each and every generation."[2]

(*Toras Menachem — Hisvaaduyos*, Vol. II, p. 251)[3]

INCREASING ONE'S TORAH AND MITZVOS

... I surely need not draw your attention to the fact that specifically after the wedding, one is to intensify his Torah and *mitzvos*. For on the wedding day there is granted from Above the ability to succeed to an even greater degree in the study of Torah and the performance of *mitzvos*.

Since this [additional ability] is granted from Above, it is surely for the express purpose that it be properly utilized in the fullest measure possible.

(*Igros Kodesh,* Vol. XIV, p. 509)

---

2. *Tikkunei Zohar*, 112a, 114a.
3. From an unedited talk to a *chassan* at the conclusion of prayers, after the *chassan* was called to the Torah, on *Shabbos Parshas Tetzaveh*, 5711.

TORAH STUDY

HUSBAND AND WIFE STUDYING TORAH TOGETHER

... The custom of our generation is that *chassan* and *kallah* study Torah together, {after their marriage, at which time there is no affront to *tznius*}, which is to say, that they connect the "sound of *chassan* and *kallah*" with the "sound of Torah" — up to and including the "five voices of Torah.

(*Hisvaaduyos 5752*, Vol. II, p. 398)[4]

Clearly it is worthwhile for you to establish set times of Torah study together with your wife *tichye* in those matters that are consonant with that which the Alter Rebbe states at the conclusion of the first chapter of *Hilchos Talmud Torah*.

I wonder why you even [felt the need to] ask this question.

(*Heichal Menachem*, Vol. III, p. 188)

A PERIOD OF TIME IMMEDIATELY AFTER MARRIAGE SHOULD BE DEDICATED EXCLUSIVELY TO TORAH STUDY

Following marriage, when one is obligated by the Torah to also occupy oneself in earning a living, it is still necessary to have established times for Torah study; moreover, to do so in a manner of "Set a fixed time for your Torah study"[5] — fixed in one's soul.[6]

Furthermore, the foundation and basis of married life should be such that the individual occupies himself full-time in Torah study for a set amount of time....

... When the foundation of married life is in the above manner, this will have a most positive effect on one's entire future

---

4. From an unedited *Yechidus* to *chassanim* and *kallos*.
5. *Avos* 1:15.
6. *Likkutei Dibburim*, Vol I, p. 7a (in the name of the Alter Rebbe). See *Or HaTorah, Nach*, Vol. I, p. 37; *Hemshech* 5672, Vol. I, p. 7.

life — for many long and good years — both with regard to one's spiritual matters (Divine service, Torah study and performance of *mitzvos*), as well as with regard to one's material matters (earning a living and the like). ...

(*Hisvaaduyos* 5746, Vol. IV, p. 440)[7]

TORAH STUDY AS A PREPARATION TO *SHLICHUS*

In order to succeed in *shlichus*, one must first make the necessary preparations. Among them: at least one year of studying Torah with vitality and vigor [after one's marriage].[8]

(*Likkutei Sichos*, Vol. XXIII, p. 540)

FIXED TIMES FOR TORAH STUDY

[With regard to] the manner of your establishing yourself after the wedding — [it should be] in a manner where you are able to set aside fixed times for Torah study to the degree that you require.

(*Heichal Menachem*, Vol. III, p. 175)

SPENDING EVEN PART OF THE DAY EXCLUSIVELY STUDYING TORAH ONLY WITH PRIOR FULL JOYOUS AGREEMENT OF BOTH PARTIES

Understandably, it is laudable to order one's life immediately after marriage in a manner that the husband spends (at least) part of the day exclusively in Torah study, inasmuch as the wedding is the inception of an eternal edifice.

However, it is also self-understood that this limits and curbs [one's ability to earn a livelihood] and slightly reduces the ability to obtain one's material needs.

---

7. From an unedited *Sichah*.

8. The above is a reply to an individual who desired to go out on the Rebbe's *shlichus* immediately after his wedding.

As this [reduction] is felt on a daily basis, and conversely, a Jew's life is to be lived — as the verse states "with joy and gladness of heart" and with trust [in G-d], it is necessary that there first be obtained a full-fledged joyous agreement [from both parties] (to beginning [mutual] lives bound up to a life of Torah, a Torah of Life).

If the two of them will both agree to this, agreeing in the manner described above, then may it be G-d's will that all this transpire in a good and auspicious hour.

(*Likkutei Sichos*, Vol. XXXIV, p. 296)

CONTINUING TO SPREAD FORTH THE WELLSPRINGS OF JUDAISM AND CHASSIDUS

I am very puzzled and perplexed at not having received any news from you from the time that you were married, although I am confident that you are filling your days with purpose and content ... particularly within the context of spreading forth the wellsprings of Judaism and *Chassidus*....

Of course there is room to say that the days preceding the wedding, as was the wedding day and the days following the wedding, were extremely busy, much more than usual.

Nevertheless, it is self-understood that a thinking person cannot permit these inconveniences to sidetrack him from the above actions [of spreading forth the wellsprings of Judaism and *Chassidus*], and [moreover,] cannot even distract him from notifying me about his accomplishments in this area.

If anything, the opposite is true, [that these are most auspicious days for accomplishing the spreading forth of the wellsprings of Judaism and *Chassidus*].

See also the *Hilchos Talmud Torah* of the Alter Rebbe, beginning of chapter three, wherein the Alter Rebbe states that even after a person marries, he retains the ability to study Torah for two or three years without much anxiety and difficulty, etc.

(*Igros Kodesh*, Vol. XV, p. 68)

STUDYING IN A KOLLEL

WHEN IN DOUBT, DO WITHOUT

It is well known that when a person is in doubt [as to whether to study in a *Kollel* immediately following his marriage,] then there is no point in his doing so. For it, [i.e., the *Kollel*,] is for those individuals who have a strong desire to study Torah and who are quite sure that they will study assiduously.

(From a handwritten response of the Rebbe)[9]

In general, when a person is in doubt as to whether to study in a *Kollel*, it is not advisable to enter the *Kollel* (where one is to study assiduously, etc.).

(*Heichal Menachem*, Vol. III, p. 178)

ENTERING A KOLLEL AFTER HAVING BEEN MARRIED FOR A CONSIDERABLE AMOUNT OF TIME

... In the overwhelming majority of instances, [beginning] to study in a *Kollel* after not doing so for so long a period, as in your case, will not be with the proper peace of mind. Therefore ... [it would probably be best for you not to do so], as is readily understood.

(*Heichal Menachem*, Vol. III, p. 178)

---

9. Printed in *Beis Moshiach* Magazine (together with a facsimile of the Rebbe's holy handwritten response), Issue 286.

STUDY IN A KOLLEL ONLY IF YOU EARN A STIPEND

It is not advisable to study in a *Kollel* if they don't provide you with a salary.

(*Heichal Menachem*, Vol. III, p. 176)

"HONEYMOONING"

I have never heard that one begins an "eternal edifice" with... pleasure trips.

It would seem that the establishment [of a Jewish home] should be upon the bedrock foundations of Torah and *mitzvos* and the service of prayer.

(From a handwritten response of the Rebbe)[10]

During present times, many couples go on a "honeymoon" [soon after their marriage]. Would only this custom be nullified, as it leads to many pitfalls and to many untoward consequences. It is truly astounding how people fail to realize how much harm can result from such behavior:

When a young couple, soon after their marriage, travels to a distant location and they are not well-versed in the laws [of family purity], they lack a *shomer*, [a "guard" or escort who is to accompany *chassan* and *kallah* during the week of the wedding,] and so on, then they subject themselves to tremendous tests.

This is so even when traveling to a city where all one's Jewish needs, including kosher provisions and a kosher *mikveh*, are available, and even when one knows the location of the *mikveh* and one is not embarrassed to ask, etc.

How much more so [is this custom troublesome] during present days, when couples think it necessary to travel specifically

---

10. Printed in *Beis Moshiach* Magazine (together with a facsimile of the Rebbe's holy handwritten response), Issue 111.

to [exotic locations] such as the Bahamas and the like, traveling to places where there is no kosher *mikveh*, etc.

(*Sichos Kodesh* 5728, Vol. I, p. 450)

Chapter Two

The New Residence: Where and How to Dwell in a City

Where to Establish One's Residence

With regard to your writing about where a person should establish his residence:

The determining factor is not where it will be best and most pleasant for him, but where he can do the most good and where his assistance is most needed.

This is similar to a medical doctor, who is to establish his residence where his help is needed most and not where he hopes to find the most comfortable life.

Truly, each and every individual is responsible for "healing" his environs, to imbue it with additional "light" and holiness. And with regard to Jews: the primary and main purpose of each and every one of them is to infuse his environs with a greater degree of Judaism.

(*Likkutei Sichos*, Vol. XXIII, p. 450)

In Whichever City One Establishes Residence There Is the Responsibility to Transform That City

... Even when only one chassid is found in an entire city, it is demanded of him that he transform it into a *Chassidishe* city.

He may well protest that he is but one individual, [i.e.,] how can he possibly conquer the whole city, especially when the city needs to be transformed in its entirety?

He must know that "*Tzaddikim* are similar to their Creator" — just as G-d does not demand more than the person is capable of, so too, with the demands of *tzaddikim*: they demand of an individual only that of which he is capable.

Since the Rebbe demands this of him, it proves conclusively that he can bring about this transformation. Were this not so, the Rebbe would not have demanded it of him.

Moreover, the very demand empowers the chassid ... enabling him to reveal and manifest hidden and more powerful soul powers, thereby enabling him to fulfill his mission.

For when the Rebbe demands of the chassid, the chassid fulfills his task not with his own power, but with the Rebbe's power. Therefore, even if he is but a solitary individual, he is able to stand up to an entire city.

...The chassid knows that spiritually, he is far from perfect. However, when the Rebbe demands something of him, he forges ahead not of his own powers, but with the Rebbe's powers — and the Rebbe, himself, is surely entirely complete.

So, no matter how insignificant the person himself may be, he carries with him the completeness and perfection of the Rebbe who sent him, a state of completion that can never be negated.

(*Sichos Kodesh 5714*, p. 186)

THE TRANSFORMATIVE POWER OF SELF-SACRIFICE

Even when a person finds himself completely alone within an entire community or city and fails to see how he can possibly draw them to Torah and *mitzvos*, the person must know that he was granted the powers to do so.

He has an obligation regarding the entire surrounding community and environs — to draw them closer to Torah and *mitzvos*, transforming them into G-d-fearing individuals, and with time — chassidim as well.

A Jew who merited to grow up and be educated by a Chassidic father, and who had the merit to see the Rebbe and hear from him words of Torah ... surely was endowed with the capacity and presented with the responsibility to have an impact on his entire community.

... In our own generation, since the darkness of exile has increased and the people of the generation have become spiritually diminished, one seemingly cannot find a gateway and a means to transform the world from "bitterness to sweetness" and from "darkness to light," especially so, when one observes how both he personally and the world as a whole are languishing spiritually.

But this only informs us that we need to work even harder, not that we are free from the task. For surely we have been given the tool with which to perform this task — the power of *mesirus nefesh.*

While our revealed spiritual powers have indeed presently diminished, the hidden soul-power of *mesirus nefesh* is even stronger in the present generation.

When we face the world with *mesirus nefesh* ... then, even a single, solitary Jew can impact an entire community, transforming them into G-d-fearing Jews and chassidim.

(*Toras Menachem — Hisvaaduyos*, Vol. II, pp. 316-318)

RESIDE IN A CITY WHERE RESIDENTS ARE G-D-FEARING AND RESIDENCES ARE INEXPENSIVE

In reply to your question as to where the young couple should reside after their wedding, in a good and auspicious hour:

It would be best for them to reside in a location where the residents are G-d-fearing individuals, and where the prices of the residences are inexpensive — at least relatively inexpensive.

(*Igros Kodesh*, Vol. XVI, p. 203)

Reside in a Place Where Residents Are Both G-d-Fearing and Chassidic

In reply to your question as to where your daughter *tichye* should reside after her wedding, in a good and auspicious hour:

Your future son-in-law is understandably correct in stating that the residence should be specifically among G-d-fearing individuals, as this is of crucial importance, and all other matters about which you write pale in comparison.

However, in these times, and particularly in the Holy Land, it is imperative that it be [not only a G-d-fearing environment, but] also a Chassidic environment.

Since our Sages, of blessed memory, have assured us,[1] "If you put in effort, you will surely succeed," therefore with proper effort on their part they will surely succeed regarding the above, [i.e., finding a residence among G-d-fearing and Chassidic individuals].

(*Shaarei Halachah U'Minhag*, Vol. IV, p. 128)

Live in a Neighborhood of Individuals Who Observe Torah and Mitzvos

Your letter reached me with considerable delay. In it, you ask my opinion or advice as to the place in which an Orthodox Jew, a family man, should choose to settle with his family.

This advice has already been given by our great teacher, the *Rambam*: A Jew must do everything possible to live in a neighborhood and in a community of individuals who observe Torah and *mitzvos*.

The *Rambam* emphasizes the vital import of this advice by continuing that if there is no possibility of avoiding living in an

---

1. *Megillah* 6b.

unsuitable place, it is better to live in a cave or in a desert, rather than in such unsuitable company.[2]

Note also that the *Rambam* speaks there of an adult Jew, of one who is not necessarily obligated to maintain close contact with a Jewish environment, etc.

How much more so [is this applicable] in our society, where one must perforce maintain close contact with a Jewish environment, especially where children are involved, in view of their vulnerability to unsuitable influences.

It should also be remembered that the education and upbringing of children does not begin at the age of *bar mitzvah* or *bas mitzvah*, but at a very early age, and that the impressions and influences received at that age are lasting ones.

(From a letter of the Rebbe, written in the year 5725)

DO NOT RESIDE IN A PLACE THAT LACKS EVEN MINIMAL RELIGIOUS REQUIREMENTS

In reply to your letter of the 18th of Av, in which you inquire as to the [religious] conditions in the city of...:

It would seem that the situation there, with regard to Judaism, is not as it should be, and it is extremely doubtful whether you will find there those things about which you write.

In any event, the position [offered to you there] does not befit a young man who was just recently married.

You should move instead to an environment of G-d-fearing individuals, observers of Torah and *mitzvos*, or at least in a location that is nearby [such an environment].

(*Igros Kodesh*, Vol. XV, p. 354)

---

2. *Rambam, Hilchos Deos*, beginning of ch. 6.

BETTER PURCHASE THAN RENT

In general, I like the idea of purchasing a dwelling rather than renting one, as it is a shame that so much money is spent on rent, when it could have been better utilized in paying off a mortgage.

(*Igros Kodesh,* Vol. XVII, p. 57)[3]

THE OPINION OF THE WIFE IS CRUCIAL REGARDING A RESIDENCE

In reply to your question with regard to a residence:

In the main, when there is a question regarding one's residence, the wife's opinion holds a lot of weight — and for many reasons.

Thus, if, in a pleasant and gentle way, you can convince your wife to continue residing in your current place of residence — especially, as you write that you are already living there for two years — then that would be fine.

If, however, she does not at all agree to this, then you should acquiesce to her wishes.

(*Igros Kodesh,* Vol. XVI, p. 36)

SPIRITUAL PREPARATIONS FOR MOVING INTO THE NEW RESIDENCE AND PREPARING THE RESIDENCE FOR PROPER SPIRITUAL HABITATION

BEFORE MOVING INTO A NEW RESIDENCE PLACE THEREIN A SIDDUR, CHUMASH, TEHILLIM AND TANYA

In response to your notifying me that you are moving into your residence this week:

---

3. For various blessings and words of inspiration of the Rebbe on the occasion of the purchase of a house, see *Igros Kodesh*, Vol. X, p. 188; Vol. XIII, p. 53; Vol. XIV, p. 379.

Surely, [before bringing anything else into the residence,] you will first bring in a *Siddur*, *Chumash*, *Tehillim* and *Tanya*.

May it be G-d's will that you dwell there in peace and prosperity, and may G-d fulfill your requests for good in all details.

(*Igros Kodesh*, Vol. VI, p. 171)

Before bringing anything else into the residence, you should first bring in a *Siddur*, *Chumash*, *Tehillim* and *Tanya*.

(*Igros Kodesh*, Vol. X, p. 408)

BEFORE MOVING INTO A NEW RESIDENCE PLACE THEREIN BREAD AND SALT

The custom of *Anash* is to first bring into the residence a *Siddur*, *Chumash*, *Tehillim* and *Tanya*. This is in addition to the custom (which I believe is common to all) [of bringing in] bread and salt.

(*Igros Kodesh*, Vol. XIX, p. 390)

THE SACRED BOOKS A HOME MUST CONTAIN

There should be found within the private residences of each and every Jew the basic books of Judaism. Included in this, and of primary importance, are books of Jewish law that apply to the daily life of a Jew, so that the husband and wife will know what is required to be done [and what is prohibited from being done].

([This is, of course,] in addition to a *Chumash*, *Siddur*, and *Tehillim* — and within a Chassidic home, a *Tanya* as well.)

... So, too, with regard to a *chassan* and *kallah* who are preparing to build a Jewish home:

In concert with their efforts to obtain furnishings for their home — "a bed, chair, table and lamp"[4] — they are to exert themselves (indeed, this should be their primary effort) that the house contain *sacred books*, which they will use for Torah study.

So much so [will the house be influenced by these sacred volumes], that the house verily becomes a "house filled with *sefarim*"[5] — included in which phrase is the interpretation that the entire physical edifice and all its accoutrements are permeated with the content and substance of the *sefarim*.

In the words of our Rabbis,[6] the house itself becomes "an assembly place for Sages."

(*Sefer HaSichos 5748*, Vol. I, p. 191)

A CHASSIDIC HOME SHOULD POSSESS THREE SACRED CHASSIDIC WORKS

It is vital and proper that chassidim should have the following three books in their possession: *Kesser Shem Tov* [containing teachings of the Baal Shem Tov], *Or Torah* [contining teachings of the *Mezritcher Maggid*] and *Tanya* [of the Alter Rebbe]. For certain reasons, however, they should not be bound together in one volume.

One should study them as much as one wishes (though let that study be worthy of the term [study]!) daily, or at least on *Shabbos* and *Yom Tov* and at certain other times.

(*Sefer HaMinhagim*, p. 85)

PLACING A PUSHKEH IN THE RESIDENCE

There is the established Jewish custom that the *chassan* receive a gift of *sefarim* — here, in this country, the custom is that he receive a *Shas* and the like.

---

4. *Melachim II* 4:10.
5. See *Tanchuma*, *Korach* 2.
6. *Avos* 1:4.

It should also be established that in the "new home" a gift that is connected to *tzedakah* be brought— a *tzedakah pushkeh*, a "charity box."

As often noted, a *tzedakah pushkeh* in the home serves as a constant reminder of the commandment of *tzedakah*; seeing the *tzedakah pushkeh*, both during weekdays and weeknights, as well as during *Shabbos* and *Yom Tov*, constantly reminds the person about the *mitzvah* of *tzedakah*.

[Thus,] even when the individual is not actually giving *tzedakah* at a given moment (because there are no impoverished and needy individuals, and the like), [the *tzedakah pushkeh* reminds the person of the commandment of *tzedakah*].

This will then serve as a reminder both "below," [i.e., to the inhabitants of this world,] and "above," [those who inhabit the spiritual realms,] that this is a home built on Torah and *mitzvos*:

On Torah — inasmuch as it is "a home filled with *sefarim*"; on *mitzvos* — by means of the *tzedakah pushkeh*, as *tzedakah* represents the general aspect of *mitzvos*.

This is why it should become the norm that when a "new residence" is created through married life, or even when one moves from one residence to another, one should carry into the home — together with the sacred books — a *tzedakah pushkeh* as well.

... Understandably, the *tzedakah pushkeh* should not be concealed because the person is — G-d forbid — embarrassed by it. To the contrary, the *tzedakah pushkeh* is one of the adornments of the home and it makes the home glisten, as it indicates that this is a residence from whence emanates *tzedakah* to all those who are in need of it.

(*Sichos Kodesh* 5739, Vol. I, p. 364)

It has already been mentioned on many occasions that we are to see to it that every Jewish home possess a *tzedakah pushkeh*, as this reminds [G-d] of the merit of the *mitzvah*,[7] and rouses the individual to give *tzedakah*, which acts as protection [for the giver].

Thus our Sages, of blessed memory, have stated:[8] G-d says, "The soul of the pauper was about to depart [his body] because of his extreme hunger, and you provided him with life. I promise you that I shall return a life for a life.

"Tomorrow your son or daughter will ... [find themselves in precarious circumstances] and I shall remember them for the *mitzvah* you performed with the pauper, and I shall save their lives."

(*Likkutei Sichos*, Vol. XIII, p. 212)

PLACING A PUSHKEH IN THE KITCHEN

... However, in order for the Jewish woman to succeed in her crucial task and for the food in her home to be "*glatt kosher*," she is in need of Divine assistance.

This in no way is a minimization of her honor (i.e., that she is not being relied upon [with regard to matters of *kashrus*], since even the greatest *tzaddik* and so, too, the greatest *tzidkanis* are in need of assistance and aid from Above.

This Divine assistance is received when one gives money to *tzedakah* for the sake of [purchasing] food and drink for the impoverished.[9]

When G-d sees that this woman has a feeling of love for a fellow Jew and she gives *tzedakah* to the poor because she is

---

7. See *Yoma*, beginning of Ch. 3 — "until Chevron."
8. *Tanchuma, Mishpatim* 15.
9. For as we find ourselves in exile, as well as for other reasons, there are those individuals who are in need of *tzedakah*.

concerned for their welfare[10] — even the welfare of a pauper whom she has never seen — then G-d will conduct Himself in a manner of "measure for measure."[11]

He will then give her *tzedakah* from His full, open, holy and generous hand, and assist her in her awesome task, so that the food will be kosher, and as a result the food will be tastier and sweeter (even in a physical sense).[12]

Moreover, when the woman will give *tzedakah* prior to preparing the meal, this acts as a sign and commemoration that she connects her food with the food of the poor individual.

It is true that she currently does not know the address of the poor person and consequently it will take quite a while for the money to reach him.

Nonetheless, since she is presently placing the money in the *tzedakah pushkeh* and she is presently thinking about a poor person someplace on this planet who lacks food, she is therefore now linking the meal with the poor person.

This is so, for in her mind she is thinking that as soon as she obtains the address of the poor person or when the "*pushkeh* collector" will come to her house to empty the *tzedakah pushkeh*, this money will go to the poor person.

This is particularly so, in light of the saying of the Baal Shem Tov,[13] that "In the place where a person's desire is found, that is where he is found."

Now, with regard to giving *tzedakah*, it is best for the woman not to rely solely on her memory ... for which reason it is best for her to make a sign that reminds her to give *tzedakah*.

---

10. "You provided him with life" — *Tanchuma*, *ibid*.
11. *Sanhedrin* 90a.
12. Since an especially tasty dish has a special blessing, we infer from this that physical taste has halachic ramifications.
13. *Kesser Shem Tov, Hosafos*, Section 38 and sources cited there.

This can best be achieved by permanently placing a *tzedakah pushkeh* in her kitchen.[14] When the *tzedakah pushkeh* will constantly be before her, it will surely remind her to give *tzedakah*.

On *Shabbos* and *Yom Tov*, when it is forbidden to carry money and give *tzedakah*, then the very presence of the *tzedakah pushkeh* will remind her that she gave *tzedakah* before *Shabbos* and *Yom Tov* and she will immediately resolve to give *tzedakah* after *Shabbos* and *Yom Tov*.

This will immediately draw down G-d's Divine blessings, that the food be kosher, etc.

In order to perform the *mitzvah* of "Love your fellow as yourself,"[15] it would be fitting to place the *tzedakah pushkeh* in a conspicuous place.[16]

This way, when friends or guests enter her home ... the *tzedakah pushkeh* will be prominent and she will explain to them its purpose. This will rouse them as well to place a *tzedakah pushkeh* in their homes.

(*Hisvaaduyos 5748*, Vol. IV, p. 343)

ATTACH A PUSHKEH TO THE KITCHEN WALL OF THE RESIDENCE

According to Jewish law, when one attaches and affixes the *tzedakah pushkeh* to the wall of the home with a nail or something

14. It is self-understood that one should be able to recognize that the *pushkeh* is not for the purpose of purchasing something expensive for oneself, but for the poor.
15. *Vayikra* 19:18.
16. If it is impossible for the *tzedakah pushkeh* to be conspicuous (because of the manner in which it is attached to the wall) then she should place an additional *tzedakah pushkeh* in a conspicuous place. Then she will have *tzedakah pushkehs* with both qualities: attached as well as conspicuous.

similar, it becomes part of the house. It is then considered as if the person built a new home: "a home of charity."[17]

Another benefit of having the *tzedakah pushkeh* attached to the wall:

Our Sages, of blessed memory, state:[18] "The world stands on three things — on [the study of] Torah, the service [of G-d], and deeds of kindness." Just as the world at large stands on these three things, so too does the microcosmic world of man — his private home — stand on these three principles.

Thus, when a person affixes a *tzedakah pushkeh* in his home, doing so in a manner that according to Jewish law it becomes part of his house — in addition to placing a bookcase in his home in a manner that according to *Halachah* it becomes part of the home and he places there sacred books and prayer books — the home then becomes a "house of Torah," a "house of divine service," and a house of "deeds of kindness."

By combining these three aspects, he adds permanence and strength to his home.

In practical terms: a *tzedakah pushkeh* should be affixed to the kitchen wall with a nail and the like. This will transform the entire abode into a "house of *tzedakah*."

(*Hisvaaduyos* 5748, Vol. IV, p. 345)

---

17. Another benfit of attaching the *tzedakah pushkeh* to the wall is that it will then not be moved to another room and be forgotten there, or left there on purpose, because it is thought to be a more important room.

18. *Avos* 1:2.

MOVING DAY: WHEN TO MOVE IN AND WHEN NOT TO MOVE IN TO A NEW RESIDENCE

BEST TO MOVE IN ON A TUESDAY

... If it is not too difficult, it would be a good idea to move on [Tuesday,] the "day in which 'it was good' is stated twice." If this poses some difficulty, you can move on any of the other weekdays (except for Monday and Wednesday).[19]

(*Igros Kodesh,* Vol. XV, p. 390)

MONTH OF NISSAN IS A GOOD TIME TO MOVE INTO A NEW RESIDENCE

... The idea of moving your possessions into your new residence prior to Pesach is a good one, for as known, the month of Nissan is the Month of Freedom[20] — freedom from all [untoward] matters, including worries and limitations, etc.

MOVE IN ELUL, NOT AV

... In light of the well-known saying of our Sages, of blessed memory, if at all possible do not move into your new home during this month, [the month of Av,] but during the month of Elul, the Month of Mercy.

(*Igros Kodesh,* Vol. XIX, p. 390)

AFFIXING THE MEZUZOS

You are no doubt aware of our custom to affix the *mezuzos* immediately upon moving into the house, needless to say without a blessing.[21]

---

19. See *Tur* and *Shulchan Aruch* and their commentaries, *Yoreh Deah* 179:2.
20. See *Shemos Rabbah* 15:1. See also *Or HaTorah, Bo,* p. 364ff., *et al.*
21. See also *Shaarei Halachah U'Minhag,* Vol. III, p. 342 and footnotes there, regarding a tradition from the Rebbe Rashab.

Thirty days later, however, one of the *mezuzos* is removed for examination, and this *mezuzah* of course may be replaced by a better one. One now recites the blessing as one affixes the new *mezuzah*, having in mind those already in position on the other doorways.

(*Igros Kodesh*, Vol. X, p. 218)

... It is the custom of *Anash* to first bring into the residence a *Siddur*, *Chumash*, *Tehillim* and *Tanya* and also to immediately affix the *mezuzos*.

(*Igros Kodesh*, Vol. XV, p. 390)

WHEN TO AFFIX MEZUZOS IN ERETZ YISRAEL

With regard to affixing the *mezuzos*:

You should inquire as to the custom in the Holy Land regarding this matter.

Our custom, that is *outside of Eretz Yisrael*,[22] is to affix the *mezuzos* without a blessing immediately upon moving into the house. Thirty days later one of them is removed for examination (or to exchange it for a better one). The blessing is then recited as one affixes the new *mezuzah*, having in mind those already on the other doorways.

(*Igros Kodesh*, Vol. XIX, p. 390)

PLACEMENT OF THE MEZUZOS

A *mezuzah* should be affixed on the right, as one faces the room into which the door swings ("*al pi heker tzir*"[23]).

This applies even to the *sole* doorway to a balcony — as was the case in the residence of my father-in-law, the Rebbe — in accordance with his ruling.

---

22. See *Shulchan Aruch*, *Yoreh Deah*, 286:22.
23. Literally, "as one sees the hinge."

This rule does not apply to the front door; [i.e., irrespective of the above, the *mezuzah* is always on one's right as one enters the house].

(*Sefer HaMinhagim*, p. 81)

CHANUKAS HABAYIS — HOUSEWARMING

HAVING CHILDREN STUDY TORAH IN THE NEW RESIDENCE PRIOR TO MOVING IN

My father-in-law, the Rebbe, once related that when he got married a home was built for him, (i.e., an additional section was built on to an existing home). Prior to his moving in, however, children from the town's *Talmud Torah* were brought into the home so that they could learn Torah there. Afterwards, he and his wife moved into the house.

A tale about an individual who devoted himself to the leadership of the Jewish people, particularly a story that he himself related, is not merely a story, but — as we mentioned earlier: the "Deeds of the father are a sign [and inspiration] to their progeny" — it is a lesson for us.

... This aspect — of seeing to the Torah study needs of small children — is the fitting beginning of building a house in Israel, that it be with G-d's help an "eternal edifice" and that the person succeed as he goes out into the world to earn a living, as well as to merit children, life and ample sustenance.

(*Toras Menachem — Hisvaaduyos*, Vol. V, pp. 40-42)

HAVING CHILDREN STUDY TORAH IN THE NEW RESIDENCE PRIOR TO MOVING IN SERVES AS THE CHANUKAS HABAYIS

There is a Jewish custom of beginning [dwelling in a home,] by bringing children into the residence, in order for them to learn there *Alef Beis* or verses of Torah and the like. This serves as a [most fitting] *Chanukas HaBayis*.

(*Sefer HaSichos* 5748, Vol. II, p. 642)

CELEBRATING THE NEW HOME WITH A CHANUKAS HABAYIS

... With regard to a *Chanukas HaBayis* ...

Since it is a Jewish custom, and moreover — and this is of greatest import — that in a Chassidic discourse of the Alter Rebbe,[24] he explains "the reason why we make a festive meal and rejoice at a *Chanukas HaBayis*," therefore this practice should be observed.

When a Chassidic *farbrengen* will be held [in the new home,] at which time words of Torah and *Chassidus* will be delivered, then it will be beneficial both materially and spiritually.

(*Igros Kodesh*, Vol. XXI, p. 282)[25]

---

24. *Maamorei Admur HaZakein — Hanochas HaRap*, p. 79.
25. Printed as well in *Sefer HaMinhagim*, p. 81.

Chapter Three

Making a Living, Building a Life

Shlichus — Living One's Life as the Rebbe's Emissary

The Obligation to Go on Shlichus

... The above serves as encouragement and empowerment to all the *Shluchim* who occupy themselves in the dissemination of Torah and Judaism and the dissemination of the wellsprings of *Chassidus*, doing so as emissaries of my father-in-law, the Rebbe, "One emissary making another — even up to one hundred emissaries."[1]

They are to know and remember that the command and directive of the *Nasi* of our generation that we are to occupy ourselves in the dissemination of Torah and Judaism does not come under the heading of "*hiddur mitzvah*," spiritual beautification and adornment, but is actual *pikuach nefesh*, an actual matter of life and death.

For the *Nasi* of our generation is standing and crying out, "Do not stand idly by as your brother's blood is [spiritually] being spilled"[2] — "... You are capable of rescuing him"[3]!

---

1. *Kiddushin* 41a; *Rambam, Hilchos Geirushin* 7:4.
2. *Vayikra* 19:16.
3. Commentary of *Rashi, ibid.*

Since this is so, surely the *Shluchim* will increase their *shlichus* efforts with even greater vigor and vitality in fulfilling the mission of the *Nasi* of our generation.

May a multitude of others learn and follow their example — that they too join the *Shluchim* of the *Nasi* of our generation — and occupy themselves in the dissemination of Torah and Judaism and the dissemination of the wellsprings of *Chassidus*.

(*Hisvaaduyos*, Vol. III, p. 260)

GO ON SHLICHUS WITH JOY AND GLADNESS OF HEART

... In practical terms and summarizing all the above:

All of you who are here should go on *shlichus*. Do so with joy and gladness of heart, and G-d will provide you with all your material and spiritual needs.

(*Sichos Kodesh 5721*, p. 198)

SHLICHUS DEVELOPS AND REVEALS WITHIN THE SHALIACH HIS LOFTIEST POTENTIAL

Chassidus cites[4] the parable and explanation of the soul's descent within a body, comparing it to a king who desires that his son utilize all his abilities and reveal his complete potential.

In order to achieve this, the king sends his son to a place very distant from the royal palace, a place where the manner of conduct is not at all similar to — indeed it may even be antithetical to — the [fine and upstanding] conduct in the royal palace.

When the prince faces all the obstacles and difficulties [in his new place] and nonetheless overcomes them and acts in a princely fashion, then all his hidden powers are revealed from potentiality into actuality, and he utilizes his talents in the best and greatest manner possible.

4. See *Hemshech 5666*, p. 380. See also *Hemshech VeKachah 5637*, ch. 70.

Similarly with regard to the descent of the soul into a body — it is a descent for the purpose of a subsequent ascent.[5]

In light of the greatness and importance of a Jew's soul, as it is the greatest of all of G-d's possessions, G-d makes it descend from "the greatest of heights to the lowest of depths" ("*m'igra ramah l'bira amikta*")[6]....

G-d does this so that when the soul conducts itself in a proper manner — that even when found in this lowly level, one can still readily tell that the soul is "truly a part of G-d above,"[7] fulfilling the King's desires — there is thereby revealed all the soul's latent abilities.

This is also one of the reasons for exile ... when a Jew conducts himself properly during the time of exile, he attains a higher level than he would have attained prior to the time of the destruction [of the *Beis HaMikdash*] and exile.[8]

The above matter, regarding the soul's descent below and the descent of the Jewish people into exile, is at times found in an individual manner with regard to certain individuals.

These people were delegated the task of descending to specific places, etc. Clearly, the intent is not one of descent, G-d forbid. On the contrary: they were provided with the power and merit to become elevated to a higher level — a level that they could otherwise not achieve — by fulfilling in that location the *shlichus* that was placed upon them.

... This is also one of the reasons why the Baal Shem Tov, the Maggid of Mezritch, the Alter Rebbe, up to and including my father-in-law, the Rebbe, all sent disciples of theirs to dwell in distant locations — although seemingly, there is no better place

---

5. *Likkutei Torah*, *Pinchas*, p. 77c, *et al.*
6. *Chagigah* 5b.
7. *Iyov* 31:2; *Tanya*, beginning of second chapter.
8. See *Likkutei Sichos*, Vol. II, p. 361.

for disciples to live than in the shadow of their masters their whole lives through.

Nevertheless, they conducted themselves in this manner, as it was specifically through this descent that their disciples were able to reveal special soul powers; they were given special merit to attain a higher level than that which they had attained previously.

Which is to say, although the disciples were ostensibly sent to these places in order to affect the places, all the same this effected a tremendous ascent within the disciples themselves.[9]

Thus we have verily observed that those who fulfilled the *shlichus* and did so with dedication and commitment and not out of a sense of compulsion or being forced ... achieved a tremendous personal degree of spiritual success.

Surely their degree of success was infinitely greater than those who dodged *shlichus*, or those who were never offered the position of *shlichus* in the first place — probably because they did not receive this *zechus* — and live close by.

(*Likkutei Sichos*, Vol. XIV, pp. 325-326)

SHLICHUS — NOW AS BEFORE

.... We must but believe with complete faith that there is no difference from before [the passing of the Previous Rebbe] to now; we must fulfill our *shlichus*.

We perceive that those individuals who conducted themselves in this manner — they did not think of matters as they exist in the realm of nature, for they know that they are going in the *shlichus* of the *Nasi HaDor* who transcends the bounds of nature — were tremendously successful.

9. See *Likkutei Sichos*, *ibid.*, p. 367.

We must be totally resolute in the knowledge that when we are connected to the Rebbe, nature has no say, and that the Rebbe can give and desires to give.

This is important not only regarding one's success in fulfilling his *shlichus*, but also regarding providing for one's personal material matters as well.

For as mentioned earlier, the Rebbe also concerns himself with the material needs of each individual, as the Rebbe always conducted himself in a manner that the material and spiritual went hand in hand.

When one opens the door for G-d, even if it is but "the [tiny space of a] point of a needle," G-d reciprocates by opening with the broadness of the *Ulam* [which had a breadth of 32 *amos* and] which was always open, providing all manner of good, both materially and spiritually.

(*Toras Menachem — Hisvaaduyos*, Vol. VII, p. 338)

PLACE YOURSELF IN THE OTHER PERSON'S SHOES AND GO ON SHLICHUS

... The above is also connected with *Rashi's* statement,[10] "Look upon yourself as if you were a poor person":

Were you to be in the [spiritually] impoverished state of that pauper, you would protest and let out a cry; you would never agree to a situation where the other would occupy himself in *hiddur mitzvah*, in his own personal spiritual adornment, and not come to your aid when you are lacking the critical and basic [spiritual] necessities.

So, too, when G-d has aided you that you find yourself in a place where you lack nothing, and you know that others are lacking basic spiritual necessities, it is incumbent upon you to travel there [on *shlichus*] to assist him.

(*Sichos Kodesh* 5729, Vol. I, p. 369)

---

10. *Shemos* 22:24.

The Tremendous Advantage Of Those Who Go On Shlichus

There is a tremendous advantage to those who travel to distant places in order to fulfill the *shlichus* of the Rebbe, the *Nasi*. For as known, there is the famous saying of the Baal Shem Tov,[11] that "In the place where a person's desire is found, that is where he is found."

Thus, although [the *shluchim*] are found in a place that is [physically] distant from the *Tziyon*, but since in that distant place is to be found the Rebbe's desire, that is where the Rebbe is found. And fortunate is their lot both materially and spiritually.

All the justifications of how difficult *shlichus* is merely conceal and obscure [the truth]. When one begins to actually fulfill his *shlichus* mission, all these difficulties simply melt away.

Especially now that we have merited (and in truth, this is not at all a merit) that nowadays *shlichus* is accompanied with ample sustenance and honor, unlike previous days when going on *shlichus* involved tremendous difficulties.

Thus we observe that when the *shaliach* arrives here everyone rejoices over him, he is elevated and given attention — and most importantly, the *shaliach* himself is happy and achieves importance in his own eyes. Moreover, when he comes home, he tells his family that he is a *shaliach* and that he was honorably received, etc.

Consequently, during present times a *shaliach* can receive true honor and imagined honor. The only thing that he must do is place his ego on the side, knowing that it is not he who is acting; it is the Rebbe who is acting through him.

(*Sichos Kodesh 5721*, p. 30)

---

11. *Kesser Shem Tov, Hosafos*, Section 38 and sources cited there.

VOLUNTEER FOR SHLICHUS

... Hopefully, from now on, a radical change will occur and each and every one will accept upon himself the *shlichus* of my father-in-law, the Rebbe, the *Nasi*, traveling to any and all places on *shlichus*.

The *shaliach* is to know that the Rebbe is together with him [in his *shlichus*] wherever he may be; even if he goes to a most distant place, the Rebbe, the *Nasi*, travels with him, and the Rebbe finds himself with him in his place of *shlichus*.

May it be G-d's will that from now on you will not wait until each of you is individually approached and commanded to do so [i.e., go on *shlichus*]. Rather, each and every one should volunteer, stating that he desires all manner of material and spiritual good, for which reason he desires to go [on *shlichus*] to a given place.

For though that location may well be many, many kilometers away in a physical sense, the truth of the matter is that specifically there one finds himself in the four cubits of the Rebbe, the *Nasi* — *imoi bimechitzosoi*, (absolutely and entirely together with the Rebbe) — even as he [the *shaliach*] finds himself in this physical world.

Thus, upon accepting *shlichus*, it will be good both for him and his entire family spiritually and materially, in the most actual sense, here in this world.

(*Sichas Simchas Beis HaSho'eivah* 5721)

"MAKE YOUR DESIRE HIS DESIRE"

...There are times when Moshe *Rabbeinu* is [in a revealed sense] not together with us, and we must then act "alone," in consonance with his directives. ...

A person may well say:

In the past, when he heard specific directives from the Rebbe, he could effectively perform according to the directives. Now, however, matters are quite different — he does not hear the voice of the *Nasi* of our generation! ... he is totally "alone" without his Rebbe!

... Herein lies the lesson: Even when we are but aware of his general directives, still, we are capable of acting in accordance to the Rebbe's desire.

... This is the overall aspect of true *shlichus*: A Jew is sent overseas and doesn't hear specific directives how to act in every situation, nor is he instructed down to the minutest detail.

Rather, in order to fulfill his *shlichus*, he must employ his innate intelligence and decide how to act, doing so in accordance with the general directives that he has previously heard from the Rebbe.

Should the question be raised (and indeed it is a good question) ultimately, how is it possible to carry out one's *shlichus* relying only on oneself, without detailed directives? The answer is that if you but toil, you will surely succeed, and your actions will coincide with the Rebbe's desire.

(*Sichos Kodesh 5741*, Vol. II, pp. 637-638)

ACCOMPLISHMENTS OF SHLICHUS ARE NONPAREIL

... How does one achieve helping all of *Klal Yisrael*; how does one help bring about the *Geulah*?

This is achieved specifically through each *shaliach* journeying to his "far corner," his "small city," and being entirely immersed in his actions of disseminating Judaism and righteousness among the limited number of people of his small city.

For it is through the amalgamation of all individual Jews that *Klal Yisrael* becomes a reality; it is the distant places and small cities that compose the aggregate of the entire world.

... No other person and nothing else in the world is capable of accomplishing that which is accomplished through the performance of *shlichus*.

When each and every individual *shaliach* will fulfill his personal *shlichus* in his designated location with the dwellers of that particular place, this leads to the salvation of *Klal Yisrael* and the full and complete *Geulah*, as all the work of the *Shluchim* are incorporated into one entire whole. (*Likkutei Sichos*, Vol. XXV, p. 335)

MAKING A LIVING
THE PROPER APPROACH

WE EARN EXACTLY AS MUCH AS G-D DESIRES FOR US TO EARN

No matter how much effort is exerted, no one can earn one cent more than G-d has ordained that he — this particular person — shall earn. One must do what is necessary [to earn a living], but one must remember that all his work is but an adjunct.

The main thing is G-d's blessing, and that blessing is earned by observing G-d's commands: Praying with a quorum (*Minyan*), observing *Shabbos b'hiddur*, (beyond the minimum requirements, with "beauty"), meticulous observance of the laws of *Kashrus*, and having children instructed by sincerely religious teachers.

(*HaYom Yom*, p. 76)

WE NEED MERELY MAKE A RECEPTACLE

A Jew who believes in G-d and His Torah surely believes what he says daily in the first blessing of Grace After Meals, the blessing that was established by Moshe *Rabbeinu*:[12] "... who in His goodness, provides sustenance for the entire world with grace, with kindness and with mercy."

---

12. *Berachos* 48b.

That is to say, that sustenance is provided by G-d — He alone is the one who provides sustenance, without needing the assistance of any individuals, which, [if that would indeed be so,] would be a matter of *shittuf*, heaven forfend.

G-d merely desires that we make a "receptacle" via natural means, as the verse says,[13] "G-d will bless you in all that you shall do." But even while the person occupies himself in making a "vessel" through natural means, in truth, all that is occurring is that the person is drawing down G-d's blessings.

(*Hisvaaduyos 5743*, Vol. IV, p. 1805)

MAN NEEDS BUT TO MAKE A RECEPTACLE

The verse states, "G-d will bless you in all that you shall do."

Man needs but to make a receptacle for his livelihood and to endeavor with all his power that the receptacle be pure of any impurity or dross of cheating others and the like. This means that whatever he does conforms to Torah laws.

Thus he becomes a "vessel" worthy of G-d's blessing in two ways: His livelihood will be ample and his earnings will be directed towards desirable ends.[14]

(*HaYom Yom*, p. 65)

IT IS NOT UNCOMMON FOR IT TO BE DIFFICULT TO FIND A MEANS OF EARNING A LIVING — TRUST IN G-D HASTENS THE PROCESS

It is regretful that you are finding it so difficult to accept the fact that you are having temporary difficulties in finding a job, although — unfortunately — such situations are quite common during present times.

---

13. *Devarim* 15:18.

14. I.e., not to medical bills, etc.

We actually perceive that which is explained in the sacred books, that the more one increases his faith and trust in the Creator of the world, the One who conducts it with individual Divine Providence, the sooner will there come about an improvement in the situation, and the greater will be the improvement. The same is true with regard to your situation.

(*Igros Kodesh,* Vol. XVI, p. 223)

G-D WILL FIND A WAY THAT YOU EARN A LIVING

It would seem that once again you are worrying, and central to your worries is the concern about the possibility that, G-d forbid, you will not be able to earn a living.

Understandably, it is quite disconcerting that you should be so concerned; surely that which is stated in Torah in general and in *Toras HaChassidus* in particular about faith and trust in G-d should suffice [for you not to worry].

(As is self-understood, this in no way contradicts the need for making a "receptacle" via natural means, as the verse says,[15] "G-d shall bless you in all that you shall do." However, this must be done in a manner of "By the labor of your palms shall you eat,"[16] i.e., that your palms should labor, but not your head and heart.)

This is particularly so with an individual such as yourself, you who have beheld miracles with your own eyes, miracles that transpired with yourself.

Now, all of a sudden you begin to worry if the One who sustains and nourishes everyone, approximately one billion eight hundred million people, will be able to sustain you and your family in an honorable and ample manner.

It would be a misuse of precious time to go on at greater length about something so obvious.

(*Igros Kodesh,* Vol. XII, p. 198)

---

15. *Devarim* 15:18.
16. *Tehillim* 128:2.

"YOU DO WHAT YOU MUST AND HE WILL DO WHAT HE MUST"

One of the Alter Rebbe's great and very close chassidim had a private audience [with the Alter Rebbe] in the course of which the Rebbe inquired after his financial situation. The chassid complained bitterly that his financial situation had utterly deteriorated.

The Rebbe responded: "You are *needed* to illuminate your environment with Torah and '*avodah* of the heart' (heartfelt prayer). Livelihood and what *you need* is what G-d must provide for you. You do what you must, and G-d will do what He must.

(*HaYom Yom*, p. 68)

SPIRITUAL SERVICE OF THE PERSON WHO EARNS A LIVING

The spiritual service of the person who earns a living includes arousing within himself the faith and perfect trust in the One who feeds and sustains all flesh, that He will provide him with an ample livelihood.

He must be truly happy and cheerful, as though all his livelihood was already in hand.

(*HaYom Yom*, p. 37)

"SIX DAYS WORK SHALL BE DONE"

... "Six days work shall be done, and the seventh day shall be holy...."[17] Our Sages note that the verse states here, "Six days work 'shall be done,' *tei'aseh*, instead of 'You shall work for six days,' *ta'aseh*."

Ta'aseh means an active involvement and preoccupation with the labor, while *tei'aseh* [the passive "shall be done"] means that the work is done of itself.

---

17. *Shemos* 35:2.

... The principle of *tei'aseh* in terms of man's spiritual service means that the work and mundane actions which one is compelled to do during the six weekdays should not be done with engrossing preoccupation, but as if it were happening of itself.

The verse says, "When you shall eat from the labor of your hands, you will be happy and it shall be well with you."[18] This means[19] that toiling to provide physical needs should only involve the hands and other external limbs. The head and heart, however, must be involved with Torah and *mitzvos*.

... This is also the meaning of *tei'aseh* — it shall be done by itself: the person is not devoted to his business with his mind and heart, but only with his faculty of action; and even that faculty of action he exercises only as much as is necessary to provide an instrument for G-d's blessing.

... *Chassidus* explains[20] that on a subtle level the mundane preoccupation with effort and all kinds of schemes in earning a livelihood is also a form of idolatry. For this kind of attitude implies that one esteems the mundane involvement, which is like an intermediary, as if it had a value of its own.

... In other words, the idea of "Six days *ta'aseh* — you shall do work" with effort, is rooted in his esteeming that work.

If he were to accept the truth that it is no more than "an axe in the hand of the hewer," he would not immerse his head and being in the work, but would conduct himself according to the principle of "*tei'aseh* — the work is done of itself."

(*Likkutei Sichos*, Vol. I, pp. 187-191)

TOO LONG A GARMENT CAUSES ONE TO STUMBLE

Since the Divine effulgence that provides sustenance is concealed and obscured within the garments of nature, man must use

18. *Tehillim* 128:2.
19. *Likkutei Torah, Shelach*, p. 42d.
20. See *Likkutei Torah, Acharei*, p. 27c; *Mayim Rabim 5717*, ch. 4.

his intellect as well in conducting his business. However, he is to use his intellect only insofar as it is necessary for the actual business; he should not toil with his mind to come up with plots and machinations.

This is especially true since it is "G-d's blessing that provides wealth,"[21] and the business is merely a garment to G-d's blessing (— not that the business is the true source of his sustenance, G-d forbid).

[Since the business is merely a garment,] we thus understand[22] that just as "too long a garment accomplishes nothing; to the contrary, it only makes matters worse,"[23] [so too with providing too long a garment for G-d's blessing of sustenance]. ...

(*Sefer HaMaamarim Melukat*, Vol. I, p. 273)

MATERIAL SUSTENANCE BY MEANS OF SPIRITUAL SUSTENANCE

IT MAKES NO SENSE TO DECLARE "I'M TOO BUSY EARNING A LIVING TO DEVOTE TIME TO SPIRITUALITY"

... *Chassidus* explains — and it is consistent with common sense as well — that there are two aspects to obtaining a livelihood:

a) That the sustenance is standing by [and ready to descend] from above; b) that it actually needs to be drawn down below into this physical plane of existence [finding expression] in children, life and sustenance.

All this is explained at length in many places [in *Chassidus* and among them, in] *Kuntres U'Mayon m'Beis HaShem Yatzah* [from the Rebbe *Rashab*].

---

21. *Mishlei* 10:22.
22. See *Derech Mitzvosecha*, p. 107b; *Kuntres U'Mayon*, ch. 2.
23. *Derech Mitzvosecha*, *ibid.*

It makes absolutely no sense for a person to claim that he has no time to devote himself to the first part [i.e., to spirituality, the spiritual aspect of sustenance as found above] because he is too busy achieving the second part [i.e., actually drawing it down below through work].

Thus, it is specifically by occupying oneself in Torah and *mitzvos* that a person's sustenance is determined and established above. [This matter is so patently obvious that] there is no need for further clarification.

(*Likkutei Sichos*, Vol. XXII, p. 378)

MATERIAL SUSTENANCE DEPENDS MORE ON G-D WHILE SPIRITUAL SUSTENANCE DEPENDS MORE ON MAN

We verily observe that occupying oneself in matters of spiritual sustenance is one of the surest vehicles and receptacles for material sustenance.

[Unlike the superficial notion that sustenance is within our hands and spirituality is in G-d's hands, matters are in fact] to the contrary:

Material sustenance is in G-d's hands, as we say in the text of Grace After Meals, a blessing of Torah origin,[24] "... who in His goodness, provides sustenance for the entire world with grace, with kindness and with mercy" — man needs only to make appropriate material vessels [through his work] to receive these blessings.

This is not the case with spiritual sustenance. Here the matter is entirely in man's hands, as "All is in the hands of heaven, except for the fear of heaven."[25] ...

(*Igros Kodesh*, Vol. XVIII, p. 98)

---

24. *Berachos* 48b.
25. *Ibid.* 32b.

WHEN MAN WILL DO HIS SPIRITUAL PART G-D WILL DO HIS MATERIAL PART

When you will do all that depends on you with regard to your spiritual sustenance — something that depends entirely on you — for "All is in the hands of heaven, except for the fear of heaven" — then G-d will fulfill all your needs, something that is dependent on Him, as it is He who provides food and sustenance to all.

(*Igros Kodesh*, Vol. XVII, p. 88)

JOB ADVICE

BEGINNINGS TEND TO BE DIFFICULT

... Since in our world all things get better with time, you should not be overly concerned if your first job will be difficult or your salary will not be satisfactory, for this is but the beginning [of your job experience] and "All beginnings are difficult."[26]

... Even if you imagine that you are being taken advantage of, as your productivity warrants a better salary, still, bear in mind that this is but the beginning.

In the above matter, the teaching "A person is [too] close to himself [to be entirely objective]"[27] also applies. You should therefore specifically seek the counsel of your good friends. After explaining to them the details and your reasoning, they will be able to offer you objective advice [regarding your job].

(*Mikdash Melech*, Vol. I, p. 236)

SEEK A SPIRITUAL JOB

In reply to your question about earning a living:

---

26. *Mechilta* and *Rashi*, *Shemos* 19:5. See also *Zohar*, Vol. II, p. 187a.
27. *Yevamos* 25b; *Sanhedrin* 9b.

Understandably, you should make an effort to obtain a spiritual position. Moreover, as you have written [to me], you have the necessary diplomas [to acquire such a job].

(*Mikdash Melech*, Vol. I, p. 238)

SEEK A JOB IN THE "VINEYARD" OF CHABAD

With regard to your earning a living:

In general, you should exert maximum effort to see to it that your material sustenance as well be derived by laboring in the "vineyard of Chabad."

Aside from the fact that laboring there is closer to the hearts of *Anash* — whether they are aware of it or not — and thus they will be more successful in their labors, it also makes absolute sense in terms of the spiritual dimensions of this matter. For our holy *Nesi'im* draw down to their disciples and to *Anash* all the material matters they require.

This is similar to the question of Moshe *Rabbeinu*, "From where will I get meat,"[28] which is to say that this [aspect of obtaining meat] was completely lower than the level of Moshe *Rabbeinu*, as explained in *Likkutei Torah*.[29]

Consequently, the actual drawing down of meat had to come about through the seventy elders. Nonetheless, this was achieved specifically through Moshe *Rabbeinu* [as he was the leader of the generation and everything that was drawn down from Above came through his intermediacy].

Thus, when your earning a livelihood is connected to the "vineyard of *Chabad*," the spiritual side and the material side assist each other.

(*Igros Kodesh*, Vol. IX, p. 13)

---

28. *Bamidbar* 11:13.
29. See *Likkutei Torah, Bamidbar*, p. 17d ff.; *Behaaloscha*, 31d ff.

GET A JOB WHERE YOUR TALENTS SHINE

In reply to your question as to what would be the best type of job for you to obtain:

Understandably, you should give priority to the type of job where you can best utilize your talents and knowledge.

Also, seek the counsel of your local good friends, as this will clarify to a greater extent the situation, potential jobs, etc.

(*Heichal Menachem*, Vol. III, p. 179)

IT DOESN'T MATTER WHERE YOU WORK, WHAT MATTERS MOST IS EARNING A LIVING

With regard to earning a living:

It matters not whether it be at a company or working for an individual — what is most important is that you earn a livelihood. For it is necessary that you properly provide — in accordance with Jewish law — food and clothing for your children.

It does not suffice for me that you and your wife are my chassidim — your children as well should be my chassidim, and for that to happen it is necessary that your material affairs be in order.

(*Mikdash Melech*, Vol. II, p. 402)

RESIDE WHERE YOU WILL HAVE THE BEST JOB OPPORTUNITIES

With regard to your personal question:

You should lean in the direction of residing in a place that will best provide you with your spiritual and material sustenance.

It is generally true that "Man does not know how he will earn his living."[30] Nevertheless, it is self-understood that the chances of finding a job are better in a place and country that possesses

30. *Pesachim* 54b.

greater and more diverse opportunity and where there is a greater chance of using one's knowledge and talents.

(*Igros Kodesh,* Vol. VII, p. 242)

DON'T WAIT TO BE OFFERED A JOB GO OUT AND ACTIVELY SEEK IT

You write that for the time being you have not had any job offers:

In light of that which is explained in *Kuntres U'Mayon*, man must make a receptacle [for obtaining his sustenance].

It is therefore inappropriate to wait for others to offer you a job; you are to go out on your own and actively seek a job, particularly since this [i.e., acquiring a job] is more important to you [than to other individuals, i.e., those who may offer you a job].

(*Igros Kodesh,* Vol. XIV, p. 417)

OBTAIN A JOB THAT OFFERS A MINIMUM OF ANXIETY

My views are already known that it is worthwhile to get a job that provides a minimum of anxiety, as is well understood from that which is explained in *Chassidus*, that earning a living should be done with a bare minimum of preoccupation.

Therefore it would be advisable for you to give thought to the matter and make an effort to slowly begin earning a livelihood in an area that does not involve so much anxiety.

It is my hope that with proper thought and diligent searching you will eventually find such a means [of earning a livelihood]. May G-d grant you success that you find such a job without having to search excessively.

(*Igros Kodesh,* Vol. XIX, p. 143)

"According to the Advice of Friends"

... Regarding matters of earning a living — [it should be] according to the advice of discerning friends. This is in keeping with the verse,[31] "Salvation lies in much counsel"; which is to say, that the individuals offering advice are to be wise and discerning so that they are capable of providing counsel. And "*much* counsel" means that there be at least two [individuals providing advice], as the minimum of "much" is at least two.

Moreover, they are to be "friends" — individuals who seek your welfare, for which reason they will give your situation proper consideration and offer you sound advice.

(*Sefer HaSichos 5748*, Vol. I, p. 240)

In reply to your question regarding the various job suggestions about which you write:

I have already told you in the past that you should act according to the advice of discerning friends.

(*Mikdash Melech*, Vol. II, p. 231)

Make G-d Your Partner

The Rebbe once told an individual who started a new business:

Maybe you'll take G-d in as your partner by promising Him ten percent of the profits, [i.e., distributing ten percent of the profits to *tzedakah*]. Take Him in as your partner, and G-d will bless you.

(*Zorei'ah Tzedakos*, p. 135)

31. *Mishlei* 11:14, 24:6.

CHAPTER FOUR

Marital Relations

THE SPECIAL SPIRITUAL QUALITY OF MARITAL RELATIONS

... As explained in another location[1] regarding [the husband's three obligations to his wife:] food, clothing and marital relations, [and in a spiritual sense, "husband" and "wife" refers to the relationship of G-d and the Jewish people]:

"Food" is that level which is drawn down within the receptacles of the recipient [similar to food that is ingested]. "Garment," [an item that surrounds the person,] refers to the flow of G-dliness that is drawn down in an encompassing manner — a manner that is loftier than the internal manner [of "food"].

"Marital relations" [a union of essence] refers to the drawing down of the Divine Essence, which is a degree that is even loftier than the encompassing level of "garment."

In addition: The special quality of "marital relations" is not only with regard to that which is drawn down below (a drawing down of the Divine Essence), but also with regard to the Jewish people, that they receive this Divine effulgence without [the concealing and obstructing aspect of] a garment.

We may say, that this is the meaning of the statement of our Sages, of blessed memory: "He who says [I shall only have relations if] I am in my garment and she is in her garment, should

1. See *Or HaTorah, Mishpatim*, p. 1,197.

divorce her and pay her the money of the *kesuvah* [that is coming to her, since he is in the wrong]."[2]

Which is to say, that the negation of "I in my garment..." implies that the drawing down of the Divine Essence is "without a garment" [on His part — revealing the entire Essence], and [the negation of] "she in her garment" implies that this revelation is received [by the Jewish people] without [the concealing and obstructing aspect of] a garment.

(*Sefer HaMaamarim Melukat*, Vol. V, p. 304)

SANCTIFICATION

... With regard to your question about the sanctification [of marital relations], etc.:

There are many who have the custom that in the days immediately preceding their marriage, they study the two concluding chapters of *Reishis Chochmah, Shaar HaKedushah*. So, too, with regard to your question, [i.e., study these chapters].

(*Igros Kodesh,* Vol. XI, p. 18)

PROPER THOUGHTS

... Performing the *mitzvah* of marital relations requires sanctification of one's thoughts, for the thoughts one has then have a profound effect [on the child that may be born].[3]

(*Igros Kodesh,* Vol. XII, p. 424)

BEFORE OR AFTER MIDNIGHT

It is extremely doubtful whether such conduct [of having marital relations only after midnight] is applicable during present

---

2. *Kesuvos* 48a.
3. See *Tanya*, conclusion of ch. 2.

times, as it leads to the person being immersed for very many hours as to when finally, etc., etc.

(*Likkutei Sichos*, Vol. XXI, p. 455)

THE OBLIGATION TO PERFORM THE COMMANDMENT

... With regard to your question about performing the commandment of having marital relations since you are [currently lacking *Shalom Bayis* in your home,] etc.:

I am astounded by the very question, since this is an obligation on the husband and it is also a commandment — see also *Torah Or*, *Megillas Esther*, p. 92d.

In connection to the above, you will surely notify me regarding the [newly revived] *Shalom Bayis* in your home.

It is my hope that you will convey to me glad tidings with regard to the above, particularly if you will exert effort [in this direction]. And "Great is peace, the vessel that contains and sustains G-d's blessings,"[4] filling all that is lacking and [rectifying] all that is in need of rectification. ...

(*Igros Kodesh*, Vol. X, p. 136)

MARITAL RELATIONS OF A TORAH SCHOLAR

With regard to the time of marital relations of a Torah scholar, which is "from *Shabbos* night to *Shabbos* night,"[5] [i.e., exclusively on Friday nights], and the *Reishis Chochmah*, in *Shaar HaKedushah* is stringent in this regard ...

... However, the following must be made known: all the above, [regarding strictures concerning the limitation of relations to Friday nights], both according to Jewish law as well as according to the writings of the *AriZal*, only apply if acting in this

4. *Mishnah*, conclusion of *Uktzin*.
5. *Kesuvos* 62b.

manner will not lead the person to harsher and more sinful conduct.

If, however, there is the slightest doubt that this form of abstinence could lead to untoward results, then it is my considered opinion that you should not act in this manner [of restricting relations only to Friday nights].

(*Igros Kodesh,* Vol. XII, p. 389)

MARITAL RELATIONS OF A TORAH SCHOLAR DURING THE FIRST YEAR OF MARRIAGE

With regard to your question regarding the time of marital relations of a Torah scholar, which is "from *Shabbos* night to *Shabbos* night"[6] ... and you desire to know whether there is room to differentiate between the first year of marriage and later years:

I have not seen such a difference cited in any place. And although generally speaking, not having seen something does not serve as conclusive proof,[7] nevertheless, in the current instance, since none of the books that deal with this subject make this distinction, then it does serve as conclusive proof.

(*Igros Kodesh,* Vol. XII, p. 389)

NEGATING ABSTINENCE

DELAYING MARITAL RELATIONS

... In answer to your question in your last letter whether you should push off the performance of the *mitzvah* [of marital relations] for a month:

You surely should not do so, particularly since matters such as these require the full assent of the second party, and in light of

---

6. *Kesuvos* 62b.
7. See *Sedei Chemed Klalim, Maareches HaLamed, Klal* 77.

that which is stated in the Codes that it, [i.e., refraining from relations,] is painful for the person, it is difficult to ascertain whether the assent [of the second party] is without reservation.

I have already written to many regarding matters such as these, [i.e., practicing abstinence,] that this "pious" form of behavior is actually a matter of laxity and even worse than laxity.

For in our spiritually impoverished generation there are indeed very few individuals who are capable of abstinence without pitfalls, etc., heaven forfend.

May it be G-d's will that you cease delving so deeply into matters such as these, for delving into these matters is improper and surely unnecessary.

(*Igros Kodesh*, Vol. XIII, p. 314)

PRACTICING ABSTINENCE

With regard to your thought about practicing abstinence, provided you obtain your wife's permission:

I am not at all in favor of this. Aside from the fact that in the overwhelming majority of instances permission is not granted with a complete heart, it is also extremely doubtful whether such abstinence adds purity and refines one's thoughts, or G-d forbid, it does the opposite.

Indeed, it is well known that "he who possesses bread in his basket" is not hungry[8] ... [while he who does not have bread at hand is in a continual state of hunger].

Since a person's spiritual status is in keeping with the feelings of one's heart (*acharei machsheves halev hadevarim holchim*), it is therefore my considered opinion that acting in this [abstinent] manner is not the path for you to take to achieve the goal to which you aspire.

---

8. See *Yoma* 18b and additional sources cited there.

See also *Torah Or, Megillas Esther,* p. 92d, [where the Alter Rebbe writes about those who mistakenly disparage the importance and significance of intimate relations], ("this is not so, for it is indeed a great matter, and [in heaven] above as well it is a great matter...").

(*Igros Kodesh,* Vol. X, p. 370)

In general, I do not approve of a person's conducting himself with such strictures, i.e., to practice abstinence. For in our generation only a select few [who practice abstinence] are able to keep from thinking inappropriate thoughts, if not worse than that.

Who then is to say [that through practicing abstinence] the person's Torah study and prayer will be conducted in purity? Thus, with regard to the overwhelming majority of people who would act in this manner, the benefit is more than cancelled out by the loss.

This is so much so, that in the situation which you describe, [where it would be dangerous for your wife to become pregnant,] the *Tzemach Tzedek* has permitted the use of a *moch* (see his Responsa, *Even HaEzer*, ch. 92).

In addition to all the above, even when the wife offers her assent to such conduct, there is ample room for argument whether she really is offering her full assent. Moreover, in many instances, the lack of intimate relations has a deleterious effect on the health of the woman.

(*Igros Kodesh,* Vol. IX, p. 327)

... What is definitely in need of rectification is that which you write that the above individual forbade [intimate relations] throughout the week and only permitted it on *Shabbos* night. Moreover, it seems from your letter that he issued his prohibition in a public and forceful manner.

The concerns regarding what such a prohibition might well engender in our spiritually impoverished generation is easily understood.

If you will be unable to change his mind, then there is a strong possibility that I will write to him about this.

(*Igros Kodesh,* Vol. XV, p. 228)

WHEN PREGNANCY IS DANGEROUS

You write in your letter about what you said to your wife *tichye* [about practicing abstinence], and she also agreed not to go to the *mikveh* for many years, as she does not have the strength to bear a child:

I was absolutely shocked by what my eyes beheld in your letter! According to the opinion of many codifiers her offering her assent and forgiveness does not make it valid[9] and thus the obligation [to engage in relations] still remains.

Aside from the above, this approach of practicing self-mortification and self-affliction at the expense of others is something I have never heard of!

If indeed it is as you write, that the doctors state that it is dangerous for her to conceive, then [in such a situation] there is a well-known ruling of the *Tzemach Tzedek*[10] (see there) that this is one of the "three [types of] women who can have relations using a *moch*."[11]

I do not wish to go on at length, since this has already been amply explained [in numerous places]; surely the above few lines will suffice.

(*Igros Kodesh,* Vol. VI, p. 157)

---

9. See *Shulchan Aruch, Even HaEzer* 76:1.
10. *She'eilos U'Teshuvos Tzemach Tzedek, Even HaEzer,* Vol. I, ch. 89.
11. *Yevamos* 12b.

REMAINING "FREE FOR ONE'S FAMILY"

TRY NOT TO TRAVEL FROM HOME DURING FIRST YEAR OF MARRIAGE

To an individual who very soon after his wedding desired to travel from his home for the Pesach festival, the Rebbe responded:

It is not advisable to travel [away from one's family] during the first year of marriage.

(*Likkutei Sichos*, Vol. XXIV, p. 468)

PESACH IS TO BE CELEBRATED WITH ONE'S FAMILY

... With regard to your question about traveling here for a stay of several weeks:

Although I do not see the necessity for you to do so, still, since you write that you already have the means to cover most of the expenses, then if you wish to do so, you may as well.

However, I do not approve of your plan of traveling before Pesach and celebrating Pesach here, inasmuch as it is the custom of Jewish men that if at all possible, Pesach is celebrated together with their family.

Since it was not imperative for you to come here until now, surely it will not matter if the trip will be delayed for several weeks.

(*Igros Kodesh,* Vol. X, p. 310)

CHAPTER FIVE

Pregnancy

THE FIRST CHILD — THE FIRST OF MANY

... One of the strongest objections for delaying the birth of the first child and/or limiting the number of children is fear of the financial inability to support children.

Naturally, parents want the best for their children, and fear of being unable to provide adequately is a powerful deterrent to having them. This is a genuine concern — but based on an assumption that springs from a weakness of faith and presumptuousness.

One who fears that he will not be able to provide is assuming that it is completely through his efforts that he succeeds.

True, Torah requires that man work to provide for his family. But it is a primary tenet of Judaism that all success comes from G-d, that it is His blessings that give sustenance, not one's own efforts alone. It is G-d who provides for all of His creatures; another mouth will not overburden Him.

But the objections continue. Granted that having children is a fine, even beautiful thing; but at least give people the choice as to when to have children.

However, can people be faulted for delaying their first child until they feel emotionally and financially able, or for wishing to space their children, to have a break between one child and the next?

This argument is seemingly logical and certainly appealing. But while it is an axiom of Judaism that man has free choice, do not confuse this with an unlimited opportunity to choose. A child is not a faucet, to be turned on at will.

No power on earth can guarantee the birth of a baby. That decision, that power, is G-d's, and G-d's alone, the third Partner in every child. The possible blessing so disdained earlier may not be available later.

Take His blessings when He offers them, gratefully, and rest assured that this third Partner is benevolent, all-knowing, Who can be trusted to know the best time.

Bluntly: it is presumptuous for anyone to see herself as the final authority determining life. Attempts to regulate life based solely on man's limited understanding are foolhardy, and the stakes are too high to risk the unpredictable.

Statistics reveal some sobering facts. Precisely in the past few generations, when the concept of family planning has become so widespread, we see the highest rates of marital discord.

Disharmony in the home, separations, divorces, ugly quarrels, tension, nervous frustrations, psychiatric disorders — the problems are legion, matched only by their severity.

Compare the present with previous generations, especially in Jewish homes, where family planning was unthinkable. The divorce rate was infinitesimal, respect and harmony between spouses legendary in the eyes of the world. And let us not forget the effect on the children, growing up in a household of peace and harmony and shared ideals and values.

The reason for the gulf between generations is simple. Man was created in a certain way, and attempts to interfere must lead to disruptions.

The human body is infinitely intricate. Disrupting its natural functions inevitably causes problems. Family planning, presented as helpful and logical, causes many of the marital problems so prevalent today.

Children, many children, are the greatest gift and blessing G-d can bestow upon us; do not let imagined obstacles stand in the way of enjoying these blessings.

(*Sichos Kodesh 5741*, Vol. II, pp. 99-108)

THE PRECIOUS GIFT OF CHILDREN

I am astonished by the statement in your letter:

You write that there is justification in the statement of a married woman of many years, that she is avoiding pregnancy because she finds her financial situation wanting. She is therefore waiting until matters will be in order [and will be able to move into a dwelling that she feels to be appropriate].

Children are, after all, a great and precious gift from G-d. Even when one hopes to receive a gift from a human being, *lehavdil*, it is entirely unseemly to say to the benefactor: "Presently, I am not interested in receiving your gift. When I will be ready to change my mind — I'll let you know."

(From a handwritten response of the Rebbe)[1]

LEAVE THE TIMING UP TO G-D

... In general, it is surely unnecessary to emphasize to you at any length that children are a special blessing from G-d, and indeed, one of the most essential blessings.

It is also self-evident that this is not a matter in which a human being can choose the right time and set up his or her own timetable.

Clearly, a Jew should not attempt to interfere in G-d's affairs. In other words, a Jew is expected to live a normal life, in accordance with the will of G-d as revealed in the Torah and codified in the *Shulchan Aruch*.

1. Printed in *Kfar Chabad* Magazine (together with a facsimile of the Rebbe's holy handwritten response), Issue 793.

He is to leave the question of pregnancy to G-d.

(From a letter of the Rebbe, written in the year 5732)

CONDUCT DURING PREGNANCY: NOTIFYING OTHERS

THE REBBE'S BLESSING

In almost all instances, the Rebbe would issue the following blessing upon notification that a couple was expecting a child:

May G-d grant that your entire pregnancy proceed to a normal and easy completion, and that healthy and viable offspring be born full term of a regular and easy birth.

(*Igros Kodesh*, Vol. XXIV, p. 77)[2]

WAIT TILL THE FIFTH MONTH BEFORE PUBLICIZING THE NEWS

You are no doubt aware of the directive of my father-in-law, the Rebbe, that "until she enters the fifth month, do not publicize the news."

As is implicit in his words, the emphasis here is on "publicizing" — as opposed to notifying those who are extremely close, not in a manner of publicity.

(*Igros Kodesh*, Vol. XX, p. 200)[3]

In reply to your question regarding the directive of my father-in-law, the Rebbe, not to publicize [the news of the pregnancy] until the woman enters the fifth month:

---

2. Also in many other *Igros Kodesh* and written answers.
3. The same content is found in many of the Rebbe's other letters printed in *Igros Kodesh*, as well as in handwritten responses. See also letters cited in footnotes to *Igros Kodesh*, Vol. XI, p. 200 and others.

The intent of the directive is with regard to *publicizing*. However, it is self-understood that the doctor must be told, and that relatives and good friends may be told.

(*Igros Kodesh*, Vol. VIII, p. 209)

SPECIAL CONDUCT DURING THE TIME OF PREGNANCY

THE CONDUCT OF THE EXPECTANT MOTHER HAS AN EFFECT ON THE CHILD

... Moreover, the conduct of the expectant mother during the time of her pregnancy has an effect on the child, which is why it is the custom of righteous women that — for the sake of their child — during the time of their pregnancy they are much more scrupulous in refraining from untoward matters and much more scrupulous in the spiritual beautification and adornment of Torah and *mitzvos*.

(*Hisvaaduyos 5747*, Vol. II, p. 37)

SPECIAL CONDUCT FOR BOTH HUSBAND AND WIFE

In reply to your letter in which you convey to me the good news that you have entered the second month — approximately — of your pregnancy:

Surely, as I have mentioned to ... if at all possible you are not to publicize the news "until the fifth month" — to use the expression of my father-in-law, the Rebbe.

I would suggest [to you the following]:

a) Surely you are following your doctors' orders — those of whom you already visited — regarding your diet, not overstraining yourself, etc.

b) Check all the *mezuzos* in your home and exchange the non-kosher ones for kosher ones.

c) Keep the fine custom of Jewish women, that of giving *tzedakah* to the fund of Rabbi *Meir Baal HaNes* prior to lighting candles every *Erev Shabbos* and *Erev Yom Tov*.

d) Your husband, the *Rav sheyichye*, should continue reciting the daily portion of Psalms (as it is divided by the days of the month) at least until after you give birth in a good and auspicious hour.

So, too, in the Prayer Before Retiring at Night, your husband should recite — prior to *Hamapil* — the 20th Psalm, *Lamenatzeiach ... Ya'ancha*. After he concludes the chapter, he should once again recite the second verse, *Ya'ancha*, and have in mind that G-d should consider it as if he had all the intentions (*kavanos*) that are to be thought of at that time.[4]

May G-d grant you an easy pregnancy; may you carry to term and give birth in a regular and easy way to a healthy child.

(*Igros Kodesh*, Vol. VI, p. 104)

CHECK THE MEZUZOS AND GIVE TZEDAKAH EVERY WEEKDAY

... With regard to your question about a special manner of conduct [during the term of pregnancy]:

I believe that I have already written to you that I have not heard that there are any [specific directives].

However, in general terms, you should check the *mezuzos* of your home, and also give a few cents to *tzedakah* every weekday morning. Understandably, this is in addition to the *tzedakah* that

---

4. The Rebbe offered the above counsel regarding the recitation of *Ya'ancha* to many individuals, as is to be seen from the many *Igros Kodesh* where he recommends this practice.

your wife surely gives prior to lighting candles every *Erev Shabbos* and *Erev Yom Tov*.

(*Igros Kodesh*, Vol. VII, p. 303)

PROPITIOUS DEEDS THAT CAN ASSIST IN BEING BLESSED WITH CHILDREN

SCRUPULOUS OBSERVANCE OF TAHARAS HAMISHPACHAH

... At times the impediment to G-d's blessing for healthy and viable children is the result of a lack of scrupulous and meticulous observance of the laws and regulations of *Taharas Hamishpachah*, family purity, (*niddah*, *hefsek taharah*, immersion in a kosher *mikveh*, etc.).

Since lack of [thorough] knowledge [of these laws] leads to their imperfect performance, a practicing *Rav* should inform the two of you all the detailed laws — with the understanding that you are to observe them from here on out.

It would be proper to check your *tefillin*, as well as the *mezuzos* in your home, that they all be kosher according to Jewish law.

(*Likkutei Sichos*, Vol. XII, p. 178)

TAHARAS HAMISHPACHAH IS THE SPECIAL RECEPTACLE FOR RECEIVING THE BLESSING OF CHILDREN

... Conducting oneself on an ongoing basis in accordance to G-d's will is the general conduit and receptacle for receiving G-d's blessings — in addition to the fact that the commandments must be performed in any case, since they are G-d's will.

In addition, each and every particular *mitzvah* is connected with a particular *segulah* and blessing, and as known, the blessing for healthy and viable children is connected with the observance of the laws and regulations of *Taharas Hamishpachah*.

It therefore would be appropriate for the two of you to be extremely meticulous in this matter, particularly since with the passage of time some pertinent details may have been forgotten. It is thus worthwhile for the two of you to review the laws again.

May G-d fulfill your heart's desires for the good, and may you convey glad tidings.

(*Likkutei Sichos*, Vol. XXII, p. 299)

DILIGENT STUDY OF CHASSIDUS

... There is the well-known letter of the Alter Rebbe, wherein he writes that diligent and assiduous study of *Chassidus* — a study that leads to love and awe [of G-d] — is a *segulah* for the birth of sons and daughters.[5]

Although you write that you have an established study session [in *Chassidus*] every Thursday night, this clearly does not suffice.

In addition to the concrete certainty that one must study *Chassidus* every *Shabbos*, it would also be appropriate for you to establish two or three more study sessions [in *Chassidus*] during the week as well.

If at all possible, these sessions should be organized in a manner that there will not be a passage of three days without the study of *Chassidus*. Understandably, all the above is in addition to the study of *Tanya*, as divided in the Study Guide (*Moreh Shiur*) according to the days of the year.

(*Igros Kodesh*, Vol. V, p. 185)

---

5. The emotional faculties of love and awe (fear) of G-d, are the male and female "offspring" of the "parent" intellective faculties of *Chochmah* and *Binah*. See *Tanya*, ch. 3. Producing spiritual offspring is thus a *segulah* for producing physical offspring.

DISSEMINATING THE WELLSPRINGS OF CHASSIDUS

... You can explain to her that her sacred work of disseminating *Chassidus* acts as a *segulah* for the birth of children, as is to be understood from the letters of the Alter Rebbe printed in *Meah She'arim*[6] and in *Ginzei Nistaros*[7] as well as in other locations.

(*Igros Kodesh*, Vol. XIV, p. 340)

INCREASE YOUR PERFORMANCE OF TORAH AND MITZVOS
CLARIFY IF OFFENSE WAS GIVEN — CHECK TEFILLIN AND MEZUZOS

In reply to your letter relating to your sister, who has been married for many years and has yet to be blessed with children:

I wonder why you did not mention whether they have consulted with fertility experts; if they have not as yet done so, they should do so now.

This is in keeping with the directive of our Sages, of blessed memory, who in commenting on the verse,[8] "and he shall be healed," state: "From here we learn that the Torah gave a healer the ability [and power] to heal."[9]

However, a Jew's physical and spiritual welfare are inextricably bound together, as they are "one nation on earth,"[10] and in the language of the Alter Rebbe:[11] "This means that even in mundane ["earthly"] matters they will not be separated from G-d's true unity [and oneness]."

Therefore, they are to increase their performance of Torah and *mitzvos* and strengthen their faith and trust in G-d, the Creator and Conductor of the entire world, that He watches over

---

6. Part II, p. 32a.
7. Part III, Section I.
8. *Shemos* 21:19.
9. *Berachos* 60a.
10. *Shmuel II* 7:23.
11. *Iggeres HaKodesh*, Epistle IX.

them with individual Divine Providence with regard to all the above.

In a case such as the above, it would also be appropriate for them to ascertain whether their *shidduch* with each other did not wound the pride of any Jewish young man or woman to the extent that it necessitates asking their forgiveness. [If they do have to ask forgiveness, they can do so] either in the presence of the aggrieved party or [if this is not possible,] in the aggrieved party's absence.

They should also check the husband's *tefillin*, as well as the *mezuzos* in their home, that they all be kosher according to Jewish law. Also, the wife should observe the custom of Jewish women of giving *tzedakah* prior to lighting candles every *Erev Shabbos* and every *Erev Yom Tov*.

(*Igros Kodesh*, Vol. XVIII, p. 32)

ALIYAH TO ERETZ YISRAEL

With regard to conceiving a child:

Making *aliyah* from the Diaspora to *Eretz Yisrael* is a *segulah* for this matter.[12]

(*Igros Kodesh*, Vol. XXII, p. 299)

MALE OFFSPRING

STRENGTHEN YOUR LOVE OF A FELLOW JEW, TORAH AND G-D

In reply to your letter, in which you convey the request of ... that he be blessed with healthy male offspring:

12. In many instances the Rebbe would advise childless couples to go to *Eretz Yisrael* for a short period of time.

It would be proper for him to strengthen his degree of love of a fellow Jew, love of Torah and love of G-d. For as is well known in the writings of *Kabbalah* and *Chassidus*, producing the spiritual (male) offspring of love is an auspicious qualification (*segulah*) toward producing a physical male offspring.

This, [i.e., the production of the spiritual male offspring of love,] is accomplished by contemplating G-d's greatness, as the *Rambam* states.[13] This will, in turn, elicit from Above many long and goodly years, and the production of physical male offspring.

Therefore, [i.e., in order to also strengthen his degree of love of fellow Jew and love of Torah] until his wife bears him a male child, he should give — *bli neder* —every weekday one or two francs to *tzedakah* prior to morning prayers. It would be appropriate for this *tzedakah* to be associated with feeding impoverished [Torah] students.

When a child will be born to him, he should name the child after my father-in-law, the Rebbe, that name being Yosef Yitzchak.

(*Igros Kodesh,* Vol. VII, p. 51)

BE HOSPITABLE TO GUESTS AND STRANGERS

With regard to being blessed with a male offspring:

There is a story that I heard from my father-in-law, the Rebbe ... with the lesson that one may merit a son through the *mitzvah* of hospitality, *hachnosas orchim*.

(*Igros Kodesh,* Vol. XIX, p. 333)

13. *Hilchos Yesodei HaTorah*, beginning of ch. 2.

Chapter Six

Childbirth

Shir HaMaalos

There is an ancient Jewish custom[1] which has been practiced for centuries, to adorn the newborn's home with pieces of parchment or paper on which are inscribed holy verses, angelic names, and the Psalm, "*Shir HaMaalos* — A Song of Ascents...My help will come from the L-rd."[2]

In some communities the custom takes the form of an amulet worn by the mother. "An accepted Jewish custom takes the force of Torah,"[3] and the different traditional versions of this practice will all bestow a benevolent glow of protection and blessing on the new mother and the newborn infant.

When these verses are hung up prior to the labor and birth, they will certainly invoke the heavenly blessing so that the labor and birth shall be easy and without complications, and afterwards they extend their blessings for a good and long life.

... Therefore, it is important to bring to the attention of Jewish people everywhere that even when the birthing mother and infant are in the hospital, one should endeavor to hang up a "*Shir HaMaalos*" in the room of the mother and the child, and if possible to attach one to the cradle of the baby, similar to the custom which is practiced in their home. For these virtuous acts are even more important the closer they are to the birth.

---

1. Quoted at the conclusion of the book *Razi'el HaMalach, et al.*
2. Psalm 121.
3. *See Tosafos, Menachos* 20b.

Consequently, it is proper and commendable to publicize this custom wherever Jews live, so that the verses of "*Shir HaMaalos*" may be put up in the mother's room and in the baby's nursery to afford a measure of protection.

It would be most appropriate and propitious to put up these verses in the mother's room as soon as she arrives at the hospital, when she goes in to give birth, and after the birth.

(*Hisvaaduyos 5747*, Vol. II, pp. 37-38)

RECITATION OF TEHILLIM

The Rebbe relates that at the time the Rebbe *Maharash* was born, the *Tzemach Tzedek* directed his older sons to recite the following chapters of Psalms: 1, 2, 3, 4, 20, 21, 22, 23, 24, 33, 47, 72, 86, 90, 91, 92, 93, 104, 112, and from chapter 113 through the conclusion.

(*Sefer HaToldos — Admur Maharash*, p. 5)

THE HUSBAND SHOULD NOT BE IN THE DELIVERY ROOM

The *Rav shlita* is indubitably correct in his ruling that the husband should not be present [in the delivery room during the time of birth].

I wonder why you even [need to] ask this question.

(*Shaarei Halachah U'Minhag*, Vol. IV, p. 39)

NON-RECITATION OF HAGOMEL

Following giving birth, a woman does not recite the thanksgiving blessing of *HaGomel*.

(Directive of the Rebbe)[4]

---

4. Heard from the Rebbe's secretary, Rabbi Leibel Groner.

A NEWBORN SHOULD IMMEDIATELY BE SURROUNDED WITH OBJECTS OF HOLINESS

It is very important that as soon as a Jewish child is born, he/she should be enveloped in an atmosphere of holiness. It is known that what a one-day-old baby sees and hears will have an influence on the child even many years later.[5]

Surround the child with objects of holiness and this will help add blessing and success to the life of the child so that the parents will merit to raise the child "to Torah, to *chuppah*, and to good deeds."

(*Hisvaaduyos 5747*, Vol. II, p. 37)

5. Thus the custom among so many of *Anash* to place a picture of the Rebbe in the infant's crib.

Shalom Bayis

CHAPTER ONE

The Importance of Shalom Bayis

SHALOM BAYIS — THE SOURCE OF ALL BLESSINGS

The greater the harmony, mutual respect and devotion between a husband and wife — particularly when both are observers of Torah and *mitzvos* — the greater is the measure of G-d's blessings to both of them for all their needs.

(From a letter of the Rebbe, written in the year 5726)

THE IMPORTANCE OF PEACE IN GENERAL AND SHALOM BAYIS IN PARTICULAR

... The *Mishnah* rules that "Peace is the vessel that holds and sustains G-d's blessing.[1] Within the various types of peace, *Shalom Bayis* is one of the greatest of all. ...

(*Igros Kodesh,* Vol. XV, p. 375)

THE VITAL IMPORTANCE OF SHALOM BAYIS

The crucial importance of *Shalom Bayis* [peace and harmony in the relationship between husband and wife] and the fateful consequences of the lack of *Shalom Bayis* is to be understood from the following statements of our Sages, of blessed memory:

1) G-d decrees that His (Ineffable) Name be effaced by [placing it in] water [in the instance of a *Sotah*] so that peace can be brought about between husband and wife.[2]

---

1. *Mishnah*, conclusion of *Uktzin*.
2. See *Makkos* 11a, and sources cited there; *Rambam*, conclusion of *Hilchos Chanukah*.

2) When the opposite occurs [i.e., in the case of a divorce, G-d forbid] — the *Mizbei'ach*, the Altar [in the Holy Temple], sheds tears,[3] which is to say, that this [act of divorce] has significant impact [even] on that [special] place [i.e., the *Mizbei'ach*] where atonement is granted and prayers are recited for the peace of *the entire Jewish people*. Divorce is thus not merely a personal matter between two individuals [it has a cosmic effect as well].

Notwithstanding the above, our Sages of blessed memory have stated,[4] "No two people think alike." In other words, despite the above [natural differences of opinions between individuals], it is still *possible* and indeed necessary that there be *true* peace between each and every Jew.

This is surely so with regard to [peace between] husband and wife, whose conduct, when in accordance with Torah and *mitzvos*, is [so meritorious that it is] described[5] by our Sages of blessed memory as [bringing about that] the "Divine Presence resides in their midst."

(From a letter of the Rebbe, printed in *Likkutei Sichos*, Vol. XXIV, p. 467)

SHALOM BAYIS IS SO CRITICAL THAT G-D HAS "MESIRUS NEFESH" FOR SHALOM BAYIS

An example of Divine "*mesirus nefesh*"[6] ["self-sacrifice"] is the law stated in the *Rambam*:[7] G-d decrees that His Name be effaced by water so that peace can be brought about between husband and wife.

---

3. Conclusion of Tractate *Gittin* (90b); *Rambam, Hilchos Geirushin* 10:21; *Rama, Even HaEzer* 119:3.
4. See *Berachos* 58a.
5. *Sotah* 17a.
6. Inasmuch as "what He does He commands the Jewish people to do" (*Shemos Rabbah*, 30:9), and Jews possess the service of *mesirus nefesh*.
7. Conclusion of *Hilchos Chanukah*.

So great is *Shalom Bayis,* that although it is known how serious is the matter of erasing G-d's name — "He is One and His Name is One — still, G-d has *"mesirus nefesh,"* as it were, and is prepared to have His Divine Ineffable Name erased, so long as it leads to *Shalom Bayis* between husband and wife.

(*Sefer HaSichos* 5749, Vol. II, p. 290)

PROPER SHALOM BAYIS HAS A BENEFICIAL EFFECT ON EARNING A LIVELIHOOD

... Moreover (and this is of greatest import, and it also has an effect on earning a livelihood), it is imperative that peace reign between you and your wife.

For this to be achieved, it is mandatory that each of you gives a little and does not insist on always emerging victorious [viz., winning every argument,] etc.

Having achieved this, you will see the fulfillment of "When husband and wife merit, the Divine Presence resides in their midst."[8]

May you convey to me glad tidings [with regard to the above].

(*Igros Kodesh,* Vol. XXIV, p. 194)

SHALOM BAYIS IS THE VEHICLE TO RECEIVE G-D'S BLESSINGS

A blessing from G-d must and can be achieved through conduct in a manner of peace, the vessel that holds and sustains G-d's blessing.[9] Therefore you must make a supreme effort to achieve *Shalom Bayis*.

Even if you think that you are in the right, and even when this is verily so, you should go about achieving your goals in a

8. *Sotah* 17a.
9. *Mishnah,* conclusion of *Uktzin.*

pleasant and peaceful manner. Indeed, this is the obligation of a Jew — particularly a *chassid* — to act with forbearance.

When you will conduct yourself in this manner, you will meet with success in all your endeavors.

(*Igros Kodesh*, Vol. X, p. 289)

ACHIEVING SHALOM BAYIS IS PARTICULARLY IMPORTANT DURING PRESENT TIMES — JUST PRIOR TO MASHIACH'S ARRIVAL

In reply to your notifying me about your upcoming birthday: I hereby bless you that your *mazel* increase[10] and that you may be able to make an ample living in an easy manner, providing sustenance for your wife and all your children *sheyichyu* in a manner of tranquility — tranquility of body and tranquility of soul.

May G-d also strengthen your imprisoned divine soul, that it be able to bring about in actuality *Shalom Bayis* in your household; it continuously astonishes me how you fail to see something that is obvious to all, namely, that your conduct — with regard to failing to work on *Shalom Bayis* — is the product of the evil inclination, which continues to gain strength regarding this matter.

I have already told you numerous times — and I will state it once again — that it is imperative that you make a supreme effort to achieve *Shalom Bayis* between you and your wife *tichye*, particularly so as my father-in-law, the Rebbe, voiced his agreement concerning your *shidduch*.

Also known are the sayings of our Sages that women are of a more emotional nature ("*Nashim da'atan kalah*")[11] and "their tears

---

10. See *Yerushalmi Rosh HaShanah* 3:8, and commentary of *Korban HaEidah*.
11. *Shabbos* 33b; *Kiddushin* 80b.

flow more easily"[12] [i.e., they have a more sensitive nature], for which reason you should be the one who gives in, particularly regarding material matters.

Moreover, if at all times during our history our Sages have spoken glowingly about the magnitude of *Shalom Bayis*, [then it is] surely so during the time of *Erev Shabbos Kodesh* — and the entire Jewish nation is now in a situation of "*Erev Shabbos Kodesh* after mid-day," as we draw ever closer to the end of our exile and the arrival of *Mashiach Tzidkeinu*.

It is self-understood that nowadays the difficulties and concealments are particularly severe regarding *Shalom Bayis*, for — as known — "Peace is magnificent"[13] and the entire Torah is one whose "ways are the ways of pleasantness and all its pathways are peace."[14]

These difficulties are particularly acute now, in the final exile, as exile itself is a result of the lack of *shalom*, as our Sages state in *Yoma* 9b.

Thus, the closer we come to the conclusion of exile, the greater is the opposition from the "opposing forces" which seek to prevent bringing about *shalom* in the world as a whole, and particularly between husband and wife. For husband and wife below, in this world, are the counterpart to the supernal aspect of "husband" and "wife."

Nevertheless, [these difficulties notwithstanding, we have been assured that] we were granted the strength to overcome these difficulties ("*L'fum gamla shichneh*"[15]). Surely, then, we are granted the power and the ability to withstand this test.

(*Igros Kodesh*, Vol. IV, p. 433)

---

12. *Bava Metzia* 59a. See also *Shulchan Aruch Admur HaZakein*, conclusion of laws of *Ona'ah*.
13. *Chullin* 141a, *et al.*
14. *Mishlei* 3:18.
15. *Kesuvos* 67a.

THE NEED TO EXERT THE UTMOST EFFORT TO MAINTAIN SHALOM BAYIS

... You surely know how great is the importance of peace and harmony among Jews, as is so often emphasized in our Torah.

The Torah is even more emphatic about *Shalom Bayis*, peace and harmony in the relationship between husband and wife. So much so that, despite the sanctity of every word in the Torah, especially the sanctity of G-d's name inscribed in the Torah, there is one occasion when G-d Himself orders His written name to be effaced by water, and that is... in order to preserve the peaceful relationship between husband and wife.

In light of the above you will find my answer to your question, which is that you ought to try your utmost not only to preserve a peaceful and harmonious relationship with your husband, but even to strengthen it and, as in every area of the desirable and good, to the point where it will serve as an inspiring example to all those around you.

Needless to say, I am not attempting to make a judgment as to who is right and who is wrong, who is at fault, and to what extent, etc., etc. But even assuming, for the sake of argument, that one of you is entirely in the right, it is still very worthwhile to do everything possible for the sake of *Shalom Bayis*.

Moreover, as the wisest of all men said, "As water mirrors the face to the face so does the heart of man to man."[16] It is certain then, that a consistently friendly and conciliatory attitude on your part is bound to evoke reciprocal feeling on the part of your husband. ...

(From a letter of the Rebbe, written in the year 5734)

---

16. *Mishlei* 27:20.

THE DIFFICULTY IN ACHIEVING SHALOM BAYIS IS THE BEST INDICATOR OF ITS VITAL IMPORTANCE

In reply to your letter of the 12th of MarCheshvan, in which you notify me that you have accepted and are following my directives regarding regular Torah study sessions and donating money to charity — however, with regard to *Shalom Bayis*, matters have only superficially changed for the better, but internally (*b'pnimiyus*) matters are still not as they should be:

I have already communicated to you in my previous letter that with regard to this matter, there surely will be difficulties and obstacles and particularly with regard to *Shalom Bayis*.

Moreover, it is particularly in this area that you must exert maximum effort, inasmuch as the multitude of difficulties and obstacles indicates that this [aspect of *Shalom Bayis*] is specifically one of your main spiritual tasks in life ("*ikar ha'birurim shelo*").

This is to be understood as well from the writings of the *AriZal*, as further explained in *Chassidus* (see *Kuntres HoAvodah*, conclusion of chapter 6,) that present-generation souls — except for select individuals — have already previously descended into this world and have now descended again in a state of *gilgul*.

The main purpose of this descent is to rectify their lack of performance of some of the 613 *mitzvos* in their previous incarnations. Nevertheless, [i.e., although the main purpose of their descent is to rectify some *mitzvah* or *mitzvos* which they failed to observe in their past lives,] they are still obligated to perform all 613 *mitzvos*.

The difference [i.e., the difference between those *mitzvos* they previously failed to perform and the rest of the *mitzvos* that they are obligated in any case to perform,] is that the performance of those *mitzvos* that they fulfilled in previous incarnations is not opposed by the evil inclination to a very great extent — only to the extent necessary for the person to be able to exercise free choice. For these matters were already purified and elevated (*hisbareru*) in previous incarnations.

However, regarding those matters that were lacking in previous incarnations, i.e., they — and their corresponding soul powers — were not previously purified and elevated in this world [and for which reason the soul descends in *gilgul*], the evil inclination's opposition [to the fulfillment of these matters] is there with [his] full force and might. I need not go on at length about something that is already amply explained [in *sefarim*], etc.

With regard to your actual conduct — for that is what is most crucial:

I once again rouse you and ask you to accelerate your efforts — and they should be very intense efforts — to achieve *Shalom Bayis*. [You should do this,] even though it will entail forbearance on your part, [but this forbearance is perfectly fine] since those matters that you will have to forego are not matters of Torah and *mitzvos*.

It is as I have previously written to you: Our Sages, of blessed memory, tell us, "a woman's tears flow relatively easily"[17] and "the gates of tears are never closed,"[18] and [moreover,] "a person receives blessings only in the merit of his wife."[19]

(*Igros Kodesh,* Vol. V, p. 39)

17. *Bava Metzia* 59a. See also *Shulchan Aruch Admur HaZakein*, conclusion of laws of *Ona'ah*.
18. *Berachos* 32b.
19. *Bava Metzia* 59a.

CHAPTER TWO
Partners in Marriage

THE FULL COOPERATION OF BOTH PARTNERS

... The relationship between [the] two people [who have married] must be consistently good and stable, harmonious and sincere, which directly affects the general atmosphere in the home.

... Clearly, in order to attain such a relationship, the fullest cooperation is required on the part of both partners, and each should be willing to give it freely; that is to say, each should give it because there is a desire to give it, rather than doing so only out of a sense of compulsion.[1]

(From a letter of the Rebbe, written in the year 5732)

MAKE SURE TO SET ASIDE TIME FOR YOUR SPOUSE

The Rebbe's long-time secretary, Rabbi Nissen Mindel, of blessed memory, once related the following:

While the Rebbe was recuperating from his heart attack in 5738, one of his doctors inquired into the Rebbe's daily schedule.

Among the things the Rebbe told the doctor was, that when he arrives home, he takes time to sit with the *Rebbetzin* over a cup of tea and converse.

---

1. In another letter, the Rebbe notes: "Human nature is such that when a person is pressured [— 'a sense of compulsion' —] into making concessions for the sake of another person — every day and many times a day — without as yet seeing any reason for doing it except to please the other partner, this is not a healthy situation, and it is bound to generate resentment and disharmony, etc."

"Upon your daily arrival home, I would recommend that you act in a similar manner," the Rebbe advised the hard-working doctor.

(As related in a *Teshurah*)

"Love of Fellow Jew" Should Be Particularly Extended To Those Who Are Near and Dear: One's Spouse

... In conclusion, I would like to add that particular attention has been given lately to *Mivtza Ahavas Yisrael,* the Campaign for Love of a Fellow Jew, among the *mivtza'im* that have been stressed in the last few years.

Love of a Fellow Jew is inclusive of each and every Jew, even the Jew who is most distant. How much more so should this love extend to someone so close and dear [as one's spouse].

I trust and pray that each of you, and the two of you together, will exert every effort in the above direction [of *Ahavas Yisrael* and *Shalom Bayis*]. Moreover, that you will do so with true joy and gladness of heart. ....

(From a letter of the Rebbe)

All Marriages Require Understanding of the Inevitable Need for Adjustment and Compatibility

... Marriage in general, even between two persons of similar background, entails a certain risk as to their compatibility and how smoothly they will eventually adjust to each other.

Even if the two had been acquainted for some time, it is no sure criterion as to what the relationship will be when the acquaintance is turned into a marriage, where the two will be thrown together under one roof for 24 hours in the day, day after day, and week after week, etc. ...

(From a letter of the Rebbe, dated *Erev* Sukkos, 5727)

DON'T BE OVERSENSITIVE — DON'T FEAR TAKING THE FIRST STEP TO IMPROVE THE RELATIONSHIP

... In most instances, the cause of such a situation [viz., the degradation of a relationship between two individuals,] is that one person is under the impression that there is a diminution of sentiment on the part of the other person towards him.

That individual further thinks that it would belittle his honor if he were the one to take the first step; particularly, when he finds no fault within himself for the degradation in the relationship.

However, in almost all instances, this [seeming distance between the two individuals] is but a figment of one's imagination — which almost immediately becomes obvious as soon as steps are taken to bring about a greater degree of intimacy.

(*Igros Kodesh,* Vol. XV, p. 222)

DO NOT ACCENTUATE THE NEGATIVE QUALITIES OF YOUR SPOUSE

Until after the arrival of *Mashiach*, there exists no individual who can possibly be perfect — devoid of all flaws. Thus, beyond a shadow of doubt, just as the one person is flawed, so too is the other.

Just as we have no desire to have our own flaws revealed and pointed out, so too should we not emphasize and magnify the faults of others.

If the above holds true with regard to all Jews, how much more so with regard to husband and wife.

(*Igros Kodesh,* Vol. V, p. 61)

"TRUE PERFECTION BELONGS ONLY TO G-D"

Following up on your previous correspondence, I am writing these lines to express the hope that the relationship between you and your husband has improved considerably, thereby making your marriage serve as a home for the Divine Presence, in keeping with the saying of our Sages, "When a husband and wife are meritorious, the Divine Presence dwells in their midst."[2]

All the more so, since both of you have merited success in the education of Jewish children, regarding all of whom G-d says, "You are children unto G-d, your G-d."[3]

It is therefore easy to envision the great merit that both you and your husband have, in that G-d has entrusted to you the *chinuch* (the training and education) of His children and has blessed with success your efforts to implant into their hearts love and fear of G-d.

In light of this, each of you should regard it as a special blessing to have found a mate worthy of G-d's blessing for *hatzlacha*.

Even if it appears that the other party falls short of perfection, and even if this view is not wholly imaginary, it should be remembered that true perfection belongs only to G-d.

Indeed, the very fact that we have all been commanded to go from strength to greater strength in all matters of goodness and holiness shows that there is no perfection in human beings, for obviously the previous level is imperfect by comparison with the next and higher level.

Moreover, insofar as humans are concerned, perfection itself is relative, in that different people excel in different areas.

Thus, our Sages speak of one category of Jews as Torah-learners, and of another category of Jews as *mitzvah*-doers. Clearly, our Sages are speaking here with regard to excelling in a particular arena, for [regarding Torah study and *mitzvah* observance in

2. *Sotah* 17a.
3. *Devarim* 14:1.

general,] *every* Jew is expected to be both a Torah-learner and a *mitzvah*-doer.

Hence, the difference between the two categories is a difference of excellence in each area; that is to say, in the first category excellence is to be found in their Torah scholarship, while in the other category this excellence finds expression in the fulfillment of the *mitzvos*.

It is surely unnecessary for me to elaborate for you on the above. I only want to emphasize that the greater the harmony, mutual respect and devotion of a husband and wife — especially where both are *shomrei*-Torah and *mitzvos* — the greater is the measure of G-d's blessings for both of them in all their needs.

This includes reward in kind — to be blessed with healthy offspring of your own, to bring them up to a life of Torah, *chuppah* and good deeds, in fulfillment of your hearts' desires for good.

(From a letter of the Rebbe, written in the year 5726)

Chapter Three

The Wife and Shalom Bayis

Shalom Bayis Predominantly Depends Upon the Wife

In the predominant number of instances, matters of *Shalom Bayis* are more dependent upon the wife than upon the husband.

(*Igros Kodesh*, Vol. X, p. 80)

The Jewish Woman as Foundation of the Home

... The role of the Jewish woman is of crucial importance, since it is she who is the *Akeres HaBayis*, the "foundation of the home." It is the wife who largely determines the character and atmosphere of the household. ...

(From a letter of the Rebbe, dated 15 Teves, 5739)

The Effects of the Wife on Family Unity and Shalom Bayis

... There are crucial moments in the life of our people, especially in the area of Torah and *Yiddishkeit*, where the Jewish woman plays a most important role.

Here the woman holds the main keys of harmony between parents and their children, parents vis-à-vis each other, and the children in relation to one another.

In this area the wife and mother clearly has a decisive role, and in most cases even a more decisive role than the husband and father. This is one of the reasons why the Jewish woman bears the title of *Akeres HaBayis*, the "foundation of the home."

(From a letter of the Rebbe, dated "In the Days of Sefirah," 5728)

AT TIMES TOO MUCH COMMUNAL WORK CAN BE DETRIMENTAL TO FAMILY AND SHALOM BAYIS

By and large, each and every individual has his or her *tafkid* (function and role) [in life], (as mentioned as well in this year's letter addressed to the general public, *michtav klali*).

For the time being, your *tafkid* is exclusively that of the *chinuch* (the education and training) of your children *sheyichyu*, conducting the household; and [your responsibility] with regard to your husband *sheyichye*. Your communal work acts as a detriment to the above.

Your participation in *shiurim* (Torah lessons) during those times when you are free from the above [responsibilities] suffices [for the time being, and you should not presently undertake anything else].

(From a handwritten response of the Rebbe)[1]

ACHIEVING SHALOM BAYIS DEPENDS MOST OFTEN ON THE WIFE

In reply to your letter in which you write about the situation in your home with regard to *Shalom Bayis* — connected to our past conversation regarding this matter. You ask how you should conduct yourself in light of the present situation:

My unequivocal opinion is that the situation depends on the good will of both parties. In the predominant number of instances, matters of *Shalom Bayis* are more dependent upon the wife than upon the husband.

---

1. Printed in *Beis Moshiach* Magazine (together with a facsimile of the Rebbe's holy handwritten response), Issue 295.

Thus, notwithstanding all those matters which you write about, I firmly hold fast to my previously stated opinion that with good will on your part, you and your husband *sheyichye* will be able to strengthen your home life through the receptacle of peace, the "vessel that holds and sustains G-d's blessing."[2]

Although our Sages of blessed memory have stated,[3] "No two people think alike," nevertheless there is the well-known instruction[4] of our sacred Torah, the Torah of Life, that one is to act with forbearance.

When you will take into account how hard your husband is working in developing and expanding the concern that he founded, which under present conditions is a most difficult labor, a crushing labor that takes its toll on both body and soul, then you will realize that it is no wonder that he may be ill-tempered and at times reacts to matters in too sharp a manner.

[When you will take all the above in account,] you will then respond to your husband's overall conduct in a totally different manner. Peace will then reign in your domicile, and as a result, blessings shall reside as well with regard to sustenance, and raising and educating your children to Torah, *chuppah*, and good deeds.

Since you write that not too long ago the two of you visited Rabbi ... *sheyichye* and the matter remained inconclusive, it is my considered opinion that it would be most beneficial for the two of you to meet with him again. Specifically, the two of you are to go together to meet with him.

May G-d will it that with the wisdom garnered through the counsel of many, you be able to find the path that leads to peace in your household as soon as possible.

---

2. *Mishnah*, conclusion of *Uktzin*.
3. See *Berachos* 58a.
4. See *Yoma* 23a; *Megillah* 28a; *Derech Eretz Zuta* 8.

Also known is the blessing of our Sages, of blessed memory,[5] "When husband and wife merit (a statement made in the plural, i.e., when they both merit, which is to say that it depends on both of them) the Divine Presence resides in their midst."

And G-d has already promised,[6] "Open up for Me [but the space] of the head of a pin, and I shall open up for you [a space as broad as] the opening of the *Ulam* [in the Holy Temple]."

The gist of all the above is, that the wife is deemed in the Holy Tongue as *Akeres HaBayis*, the mainstay of the home; the main conduct of the home — in a general sense — depends on her, as well as the degree of peace and harmony that dwells in the home in particular.

"There is nothing that can stand in the way of one's will."[7] I do not intend to imply by this that — as you expressed in your letter — that you are to suffer afflictions, Heaven forfend, as long as you remain married.

Rather, [my intention is] that you overcome the blandishments of the evil inclination, and together with your husband build a home in Israel in a good and auspicious hour — a home filled with peace and blessings, and one which prompts others in your environs to act in a similar manner.

I await glad tidings from you, in which you declare that you have decided with the utmost force and vigor to do all that depends on you in fulfilling that which I mentioned above. May G-d grant you success.

(*Igros Kodesh,* Vol. X, p. 80)

---

5. *Sotah* 17a.
6. See *Shir HaShirim Rabbah* 5:3; *Tanchuma* (Buber), *Toldos* 18.
7. Cf. *Zohar*, Vol. II, p. 162b.

THE EFFECTS OF THE JEWISH WOMAN ON FAMILY UNITY

The Jewish people began with one family, that of our father Avraham, and ever since then the Jewish family has been the foundation of our people.

In the family, too, each member is a separate individual, with a particular function and purpose in life assigned to him and her by *Hashgachah Peratis*, by individual Divine Providence. Unless there is unity in the family, there can be no unity of the Jewish people.

How is family unity achieved? ... When all the members of the family accept the *One* Torah from the *One* G-d in such a way that the Torah and *mitzvos* are the only essential things, and all other things are merely secondary and have significance only insofar as they are related to the essence — then there is true unity in the family.

In attaining this family unity — bearing in mind also that Jewish families are the component parts of the Jewish people, hence the basis of the unity of *Klal Yisrael*, as mentioned above — the Jewish mother and daughter have a most important part, as they both are mainstays of the home, a point that has been underscored on previous occasions.

Needless to say, the said unity must be a constant one, without interruptions. This is to say, it must be expressed not only on certain days of the year, or certain hours of the day, but in every day of the year, and in every hour of the day.

(From a letter of the Rebbe, dated *Lag BaOmer*, 5731)

THE HOME AND THE HOME ATMOSPHERE LARGELY THE DOMAIN OF THE WIFE

The Torah portion *Bechukosai* begins with the Divine promise: "If you will walk in My statutes, and keep My *mitzvos* and do them" — then G-d will bestow all the blessings mentioned further on in the portion.

The question that poses itself is obvious: Surely G-d's *mitzvos* must be fulfilled not for the sake of material rewards, but for their own sake, because G-d commanded them.

With regard to the actual reward, the reward for the performance of Torah and *mitzvos* is sure to come as a matter of course [but this should not be the main intent in their performance], since the *mitzvos* were given for the benefit of the doer, both in this life and in the eternal life that follows.

One of the many answers — as also explained at length in the *Ramban* — is that while the *mitzvos* must indeed be fulfilled unconditionally and without regard for reward, there are inevitably various distractions and difficulties connected with the material aspects of daily life.

When such distractions are at a minimum, it requires no special effort to carry out the *mitzvos* fully and completely. But when material circumstances are not quite so satisfactory, though the same performance of the *mitzvos* is expected, it requires a greater effort, for it is obviously harder to concentrate on Torah and *mitzvos* when one has to overcome outside pressures.

Thus, G-d's promise of material rewards is not meant to provide the reason for keeping the Torah and *mitzvos*, but is a promise that where there is a firm resolve to walk in G-d's way and keep His *mitzvos*, He will make it easier [to fulfill His commandments] by providing all of one's material needs and by reducing outside pressures to a minimum.

The above focuses immediate attention on the home and the home atmosphere, which is largely the domain of the wife and mother, the *Akeres HaBayis*.

Even when things seem not at all as one desires, or even if, G-d forbid, this is not just a product of one's imagination, it is largely up to the *Akeres HaBayis* to ensure that the home should at all times be permeated with the light of Torah and *mitzvos*, in an atmosphere of peace and harmony and joy, for the benefit of the whole family. For it is in the home that the husband and children find comfort and inspiration to deal with the pressures outside the home — at business and in school.

Since this great privilege and responsibility has been given to the *Akeres HaBayis*, it is certain that the ability has been given to her to carry this out fully, as it has also been given to the Jewish daughters who are preparing themselves to take their place as *Akeres HaBayis*.

(From a letter of the Rebbe, dated "In the Days of Sefirah," 5738)

THE EFFECTS OF A SPIRITUAL PILGRIMAGE ON SHALOM BAYIS

I received your letter in which you discuss the question of your husband's trip, which has entailed certain difficulties [with regard to *Shalom Bayis*, etc.], and you ask my opinion whether the trip was justified.

Let me begin with some brief introductory observations:

In the view of our Torah which is called *Toras Chayim*, the "Law of Life," and especially as emphasized in the teachings of the Baal Shem Tov, the founder of *Chassidus*, whose 200th anniversary of his demise we have recently observed, a husband and wife are not two separate entities, but are one.

As in the case of the physical body, when any part is strengthened and invigorated, it automatically adds vigor and strength to all the other parts. How much more so is this the case with a husband and wife who have been married *K'das Moshe v'Yisrael* ["according to the laws of Moses and Israel," wherein] the benefit to one benefits both.

Therefore, there can be no question that the benefit that your husband expected to derive from this trip — and I trust he unquestionably did derive it — will be fully shared by you and the rest of the family.

Another point is that the Jewish festivals in general, and those of the month of Tishrei in particular, have lasting benefits. Similarly, the Festivals of Sukkos, Shemini Atzeres and Simchas Torah, which are the "Season of our Rejoicing," are not intended to bring true joy and inspiration only during these days, and when they are over they are forgotten.

Rather, their purpose and intent is that the Jew should draw from them stores of joy and inspiration to last him throughout the year and every day of the year.

Since this joy and inspiration is related and connected to Torah and *mitzvos*, it follows that this joy truly permeates one's entire being and serves as the font for a harmonious and happy Jewish life.

Add to this the fact that one's state of mind is a powerful factor and force, not only with regard to one's spiritual life, but also one's physical and material life. For it is a matter of common experience that when one goes about his affairs in a happy frame of mind, with faith and confidence, he is bound to be more successful.

Applying all the above to your Jewish family life, it is well to bear in mind that at all times, and especially in our time, it is not a simple matter to set up a truly harmonious Jewish life. A young couple inevitably experiences certain difficulties, trials, and sometimes even crises.

However, when one realizes that these are only trials designed to strengthen the foundations of the home, which is to be an everlasting edifice (*binyan adei ad*), and as the Torah states, "For

G-d tries you to make known your love [for Him] etc." (*Devarim* 13:4), one appreciates them in their true perspective.

For, in sending these difficulties and trials, G-d also provides the capacity to overcome them. Far from being discouraged by such difficulties, they should be considered as challenges that are meant to be overcome, so that we can reap the benefits that are inherent in them.

Finally, human nature is such that when one has various problems to cope with, it is more difficult to cope with them in isolation; it is much easier to overcome them by being part of an environment and belonging to a society that is permeated with the same approach and the same way of thinking. (Incidentally, this is one of the reasons why certain things in Jewish life require the presence of at least a *Minyan* of ten people.)

After all the above observations, you should consider the fact that your husband has been given the very important function of being connected with the cause of *Chinuch al Taharas HaKodesh*, educating Jewish children in a pure and holy way, and the general development of ... which has great promise for the future.

In addition, your recent settlement in the town of ... also requires special reserve of strength and capacities. The more one is equipped with faith in G-d, confidence and joy, the better one can cope with all these problems.

Your husband's visit here brought him into personal contact with other young men similarly situated, and in some cases even with more difficult problems, and the mutual benefit derived from such contact is simply inestimable.

Even if the trip entailed certain personal sacrifices on his part as well as on your own, these sacrifices will be more than compensated by the benefits — not only in terms of spiritual benefits but also in terms of material benefits, as indicated above.

... It will gladden me to hear good news from you in connection with all the above.

(From a letter of the Rebbe, dated 25 Tishrei, 5721)

A Husband's Tireless Efforts for the Sake of Judaism Should Not Inhibit Shalom Bayis

In reply to your letter from the end of Shevat, in which you write about your husband *shlita's* work habits [i.e., his working constantly and unflaggingly] since he returned from [a visit] here:

You note the [untoward] effect this has had with regard to the family, since he is so occupied, etc. Moreover, you note that even among *Anash*, people are taken aback by his manner of conduct.

First and foremost, I must repudiate your latter complaint [that community members are taken aback by his manner of conduct]:

The very foundation and beginning of all four sections of the *Shulchan Aruch* is that "one should not be mortified by those who mock [and scoff at their proper manner of conduct]."

This is particularly so when the possibility exists that the reason for their scoffing is envy and the like. Would only there be [the true and proper manner of envy]: "Envy of scholars leads to an increase in wisdom."[8]

With regard to your actual grievance: Understandably, you are by and large correct [in your statement] that a husband and father should devote time to his wife and children, as it is patently obvious that this *mitzvah* is no less important than any of the other *mitzvos* of our sacred Torah.

Also well known is the statement of the *Rebbe* (*Rashab*) *Nishmaso Eden*, who when speaking of the above [matter of

---

8. *Bava Basra* 22a.

devoting time to one's children] commented: "Just as wearing *tefillin* ... so too...."[9]

However, it is also true that whenever one embarks on a new field of endeavor and one desires that it be firmly grounded and enduring, it is impossible to condense the [necessary] time and merely clock in and clock out.

If this is so regarding all individuals, how much more so with regard to your husband *sheyichye*, who as you well know does not believe in doing things half-way — when he embarks on a new project, he does so with all his passion and if his work is curtailed in *any* way, he will not undertake the project at all.

However, according to my estimation — and I'm quite sure that it is correct — as soon as he concludes the first stage of his labors in the new projects, he will surely enter into an established routine and begin fulfilling his sacred task as a husband and father.

Moreover, this conduct [as a husband and father] will in no way act as a detriment to his success as he labors in his new fields of endeavors. Concerning the above, there is the [following] well-known example:

Although G-d granted us numerous *mitzvos* — 613 in number — nevertheless, not only does one *mitzvah* neither detract nor contradict another *mitzvah*, but moreover, "One *mitzvah* brings about another."[10]

As to your question, "What is to be my lot?" Would only there be more Jewish women like you, women whose husbands

9. The complete quote: "Just as wearing *tefillin* every day is a *mitzvah* commanded by the Torah regardless of his standing in Torah, whether deeply learned or simple, so too is it an absolute duty for every person to spend a half-hour every day thinking about the Torah-education of children, and to do everything in his power — and beyond his power — to inspire children to follow the path along which they are being guided." — *HaYom Yom*, p. 13.

10. *Avos* 4:2.

merit occupying themselves in the education of Jewish children and drawing them closer to their Father in Heaven.

The rewards — both material as well as spiritual — for those who conduct themselves in the above manner [of occupying themselves in the education of Jewish children,] and the rewards of the entire family, particularly the wife who assists the husband along this path, is beyond description.

(*Igros Kodesh,* Vol. XVI, p. 358)

NOT BEING APPRECIATED SHOULD NOT BE A REASON FOR DIMINUTION OF SHALOM BAYIS

... I read with attentiveness that which you wrote at the conclusion of your letter about your feelings — that after having invested so much energy, strength and time in building and establishing your lives together, your family life, etc., your efforts are seemingly unacknowledged and unappreciated. This is particularly rankling since these efforts have been your constant stress and emphasis for so many years.

You surely know — having both received it as a tradition as well as having studied this on your own — that in our Torah, the Torah of Truth, the Jewish woman's role in the home is denoted as "*Akeres HaBayis,*" the mainstay and foundation of the home.

It is seemingly strange that although all agree that the existence of the entire building depends on the foundation upon which it is built — on its strength and immunity to all possible changes etc., etc. — nevertheless, nobody pays particular attention to the foundation except during the time when the foundation is put down.

Even then, those who speak about the foundation are the contractor, the architect and the builder, [and even they speak about it but briefly] — while at the same time they speak at such great length and in such glowing terms about the external beauty of the building, the internal beauty of the walls and ceiling, the tasteful furnishings and pictures, etc.

Even when someone will come along and explain that the foundation is what is most important — [i.e.,] the walls, the ceiling, the floor and all the contents of the home all depend on the foundation — and everybody will admit that this is indeed so, nonetheless they will immediately continue to speak of all the other facets of the home [and ignore the foundation].

The consolation implicit in the above analogy [of a physical foundation to the woman as the foundation of the home,] is not only that a similarity exists [between the two].

Rather, it teaches us that the lack of recognition and verbal appreciation, etc., is not at all an indication that anyone doubts the matter [i.e., that there is a lack of appreciation of the wife as foundation of the home].

It is merely that it is the nature of man that that which is acknowledged and well known does not beguile the eyes (the eyes of man) and does not arouse interest and the like, which is why people do not find it necessary to speak about this at length or at all.

With blessings for success in your responsibility as *Akeres HaBayis*, and that you accomplish this with a feeling of satisfaction, as well as blessing for success in all your affairs.

(*Nitzutzei Or*, p. 56)

TIME SPENT IN LENGTHY SHABBOS PRAYER SHOULD SERVE AS SOURCE OF JOY, NOT FRICTION

In reply to your letter of Tishrei 27, in which you notify me about the [*Shalom Bayis*] situation that has arisen between your sister [and her husband,] your brother-in-law, that it is not as it should be:

Understandably, I shall fulfill your request of writing a letter to your brother-in-law to help strengthen the *Shalom Bayis* situation. However, you on your part, as well as other members of your family should explain to your sister the following:

When a husband returns late from his store or office from whence he earns his living and derives his sustenance, no one becomes angry with him. Quite the contrary, they are pleased that the household has a source of revenue and the husband is faithfully discharging his duties as a provider.

The source of satisfaction with the husband's work lies in his having a "guaranteed" source of income, although in point of fact the employer who pays his wages as well as the actual job are but mediums and conduits through which G-d, who sustains and provides a livelihood to all, provides this individual and his family with sustenance.

This being the case, how much more so should the wife be joyful when her husband faithfully serves the "true and sole Boss" responsible for a person's sustenance, by petitioning Him in prayer — the appropriate time for personal petitions — for the family's needs.

[Moreover, not only is prayer the time for petition, but] through prayer — one of the aspects of Torah and *mitzvos* — one creates the conduits and vessels through which G-d directs the flow of sustenance [to each and every individual].

... Just as your sister does not complain that her husband is at his job or studies for many hours during the weekdays, she surely shouldn't complain that on the day of *Shabbos* he spends many hours in prayer and seclusion with G-d, for it is specifically from the *Shabbos* day — as the *Zohar* states[11] — that the rest of the week is blessed.

---

11. *Zohar*, Vol. II, p. 63b, 88a.

Thus it is stated in *Sefarim* that the prayers of *Shabbos* incorporate all the prayers of the rest of the days of the week, weekday prayers that have as their intermediary blessings [in the *Amidah*] not only "... who graciously bestows knowledge" [i.e., spiritual requests,] but also "Hear our voice..." [i.e., all manner of requests, material as well as spiritual].

... I need not go on at length, for it is my hope that the above few lines will be effective in rectifying the situation at the earliest possible time, and that I will [shortly] be receiving glad tidings [about the improvement in *Shalom Bayis*].

(*Igros Kodesh,* Vol. X, p. 57)

A WIFE NEEDS TO BE PARTICULARLY SENSITIVE WHEN HER HUSBAND FACES STRESS

I surely need not draw your attention to the fact that the conduct of a home in general, and particularly the relationship between husband and wife depends to a greater and larger extent on the wife than on the husband.

This is in keeping with the verse in *Tanach:*[12] "A woman's wisdom constructs her home" — the very structure and ongoing preservation of the household depends on the woman's wisdom.

This is particularly so regarding life in America, where a man's work is associated with much stress and haste and the wife's obligation is even greater to see to it that husband and wife enjoy a maximum of peace and serenity. The wife is able to achieve this by demonstrating the utmost measure of consideration and understanding.

[This is so] even when you imagine — and you may even be partially correct — that your husband should be capable of possessing and demonstrating additional fine qualities. For it is

12. *Mishlei* 14a.

necessary to take into consideration that this *shidduch* has been decreed in heaven by G-d so very long ago.

We observe that when one finds a fault in one's *self*, the proper path is not that of causing oneself pain over the fault, but to find a painless means to rectify the fault. Similarly and to an even greater extent should this be the case with regard to husband and wife [i.e., with finding faults in one's spouse].

For in the final analysis, it is difficult to know what problems your husband is currently experiencing, as well as the difficulties he experienced in previous years.

When, however, he perceives his wife's tenderness, warm feelings and strong faith in G-d, then one views the entire world in a different light [and his behavior changes for the better as well].

[When you will act in this manner,] then you will recognize that G-d is the Master of the entire world, particularly your own home and environment. This cognizance will assure that you will be in a better mood and in better spirits.

You will then realize that such positive behavior is beneficial for your *own self*, for such conduct generates affection and calm —much more than the amount of strain it cost for you to be forbearing and forgiving.

Hopefully with regard to you and your husband this entire consideration is unnecessary, since you conduct your home as a proper *Chassidisher* home, permeated with *Ahavas Yisrael* (love of a fellow Jew). [Surely, you realize that], *Ahavas Yisrael* is of particular importance in a *Chassidisher* home, since our holy *Rebbeim* had total self-sacrifice to make certain that Chassidic homes be permeated with *Ahavas Yisrael.*

Merely, since there is no limit to goodness [thus, although I am certain that you already conduct your home with *Shalom Bayis Ahavas Yisrael,*] I anticipate that these few lines will effect that the mutual positive *Shalom Bayis* and caring relationship between you and your husband will become even better and stronger.

This will affect not only yourselves, but will also have an effect on your surroundings, inasmuch as the relationship between the two of you will serve as a model of peace and illumination to others as well.

May G-d bless you with success.

(*Igros Kodesh*, Vol. IX, p. 119)

TO ACHIEVE SHALOM BAYIS DON'T NAG — ACT WITH TOLERANCE AND FORBEARANCE

Concerning that which you write with regard to your husband and the [present unsatisfactory] situation of *Shalom Bayis*:

It would be advisable for you to gloss over those particular matters that you deem to be faults of his. For even if these are truly faults, nevertheless, in these [later] years and at this [relatively advanced] age, it will be difficult to change him.

Harping on his faults and repeatedly bringing them to his attention merely serves to exacerbate the situation, as he finds it extremely difficult to change his ways. It only serves to irritate and anger him and leads to no useful purpose.

When, however, he will see that you show tolerance and forbearance and it does not affect your relationship with him, then within a relatively short span of time you will see an improvement in the state of *Shalom Bayis*.

(*Igros Kodesh*, Vol. VI, p. 156)

SHALOM BAYIS PROBLEMS SHOULD NOT LEAD TO NOT IMMERSING IN MIKVEH

... You write that [because of the dismal state of *Shalom Bayis* in your home] it has been many months since you have immersed in a *mikveh* and that you are not living with your husband in the manner of a Jewish husband and wife.

This conduct is not at all good. You should be strong in your faith in Blessed and Exalted G-d, secure in the knowledge that if you but observe the laws and statutes of *Taharas Hamishpachah* according to the dictates of our Torah, the Torah of Life, then this will draw down and increase the measure of *Shalom Bayis* in your household.

The increased degree of *Shalom Bayis* will also cause an increase in blessings and success, including strengthening the health of your children.

(*Igros Kodesh*, Vol. X, p. 366)

GETTING ALONG WITH ONE'S MOTHER-IN-LAW

"If you will be at peace with your mother-in-law," the Rebbe once told a Jewish lady during his distribution of "dollars" for *tzedakah*, "then there will be peace in your entire family, your entire environs, your entire city and in the entire world."

(*V'Yaseim Lecha Shalom*, p. 182)

CHAPTER FOUR

The Husband and Shalom Bayis

A HUSBAND SHOULD DISPLAY EXTREME SENSITIVITY

... You are indeed correct concerning that which you write with regard to....

Nevertheless, we have been particularly warned about *ona'ahs ishto*, "not to cause one's wife pain through one's words," (see conclusion of *Hilchos Ona'ah* in *Shulchan Aruch Admur HaZakein*) for they are tender by nature.

You should therefore see that ... appeases his wife through other means as well, not merely through logical and intellectual arguments.

(*Igros Kodesh*, Vol. XVIII, p. 525)

A HUSBAND SHOULD BE PARTICULARLY SENSITIVE TO HIS WIFE'S HONOR AND FEELINGS WHEN THERE ARE SHALOM BAYIS PROBLEMS

In reply to your letter of the 24th of Sivan, in which you write about the *Shalom Bayis* situation in your son's home [that it is in need of much improvement]:

Generally, it is customary only to respond about such matters to the person who is experiencing the problems, since only he can provide all the necessary details, while others — to use the expression of our Sages — "do not know what is in the other person's heart."[1]

---

1. *Pesachim* 54b.

Nevertheless, because of the importance of the matter and also because of your importance and honor, I will express my opinion in this matter.

[My opinion is] based on the ruling of our Torah, the Torah of Life, that peace in general is great and especially peace between husband and wife. When there are differences of opinion between them, then there is also to be found a detailed directive:

This directive (cited at the conclusion of the laws of *Ona'ah* of *Rabbeinu HaZakein, Baal HaTanya v'haShulchan Aruch*) is that one must be very careful not to cause his wife any pain ... to be very sensitive to her honor, etc.

And as is to be understood from your letter, [the problems between your son and his wife] are not at all concerning matters of *Yiras Shamayim* [where he would feel that he has to stand on principle, etc.] — to the contrary, she is very religious and observes Torah and *mitzvos*, etc.

May G-d will it that His peace reign in your son's house and may there be a multitude of peace there — something that leads to a multitude of blessing (see conclusion of *Esther Rabbah*).

... With honor and blessing that you be able to convey glad tidings with regard to all the above.

(*Igros Kodesh,* Vol. XXII, p. 258)

ACQUIESCENCE AND A GOOD FAITH EFFORT GREATLY ASSIST IN ACHIEVING SHALOM BAYIS

In reply to your letter from Sunday, in which you write about the [unsatisfactory] *Shalom Bayis* situation:

In such instances one must see to it that true friends should intervene and revive the *Shalom Bayis*.

It is self-understood that you on your part must undertake — not only promise, but actually carry out — to acquiesce to all her just demands. Should there be matters that are not sufficiently clearly justified, then the two of you should rely on the opinion of neutral parties.

In most instances, when the wife discerns that her husband is serious about and is making a good faith effort to achieve *Shalom Bayis* and is ready to yield, this itself brings about closeness between husband and wife.

As known from the multitude of sayings of our Sages, in order to achieve *Shalom Bayis* it is worthwhile to yield and accede to many things, even acceding to things [which, while they are not matters of law, they are however] above and beyond the letter of the law.

May G-d help that in the near future you be able to relate glad tiding with regard to the above.

As a receptacle for G-d's speedy assistance in the above, it would be most appropriate that immediately after your daily morning prayers you should say the portion of Psalms — as they are divided into the days of the month. Additionally, prior to your weekday prayers you should give a few cents for *tzedakah*.

Continue doing the above — *bli neder* — until the coming *Rosh HaShanah*.

(*Igros Kodesh*, Vol. XII, p. 397)

THE PARTICULAR NEED FOR THE HUSBAND NOWADAYS TO ACT TOWARD HIS WIFE WITH AFFECTION AND SENSITIVITY

... When one thinks of one's wife, one should always remember that the Congregation of Israel as a whole and every Jew in particular is deemed to be the "wife" of the King of kings, Blessed G-d.

[In our prayers,] we petition G-d that He conduct Himself with the Congregation of Israel — whom He calls "My wife" — in a manner wherein He fulfills their hearts' desires for the good. It is also well known that our manner of service below [*isarusa d'letata*] arouses a reciprocal response from above [*isarusa dile'eila*].

Thus, it is incumbent for a husband to conduct himself in a like manner with regard to his wife. For as the *Gemara* states [with regard to the proper conduct and feeling towards one's wife]:[2] "... [He loves his wife as himself and] honors her more than himself."

This is especially so, when one ponders that we presently find ourselves at the conclusion of *galus* and we are close to the imminent Redemption, about which time it is written,[3] "A woman shall encompass a man."

Bearing the above in mind inevitably leads to a feeling of honor and sensitivity towards one's wife, viewing her in her true light — as "a daughter of Avraham, Yitzchak and Yaakov."

Even if she should possess a fault, quite often this fault results from her husband's conduct —causing her to act as "the wife of a thief" [who acts "like a thief"],[4] rather than her acting as "the wife of a *chaver*" (a pious individual) who acts "like a *chaver*."[5]

(*Igros Kodesh*, Vol. VI, p. 201)

The Particular Need for the Husband To Act Toward His Wife With Sensitivity At the Time of the Cessation of the Menses

Almost all Jews have dissimilar opinions — similar to those differences in opinion between you and your wife. The reason for this is that G-d desired — and in this matter He created man — that no two people think alike.[6]

---

2. *Yevamos* 62b.
3. *Yirmeyahu* 31:22.
4. *Yerushalmi Kesuvos* 2:9.
5. *Shavuos* 30b; *Avodah Zarah* 39a.
6. See *Berachos* 58a.

At the time of the beginning of the cessation of the menses it is common that all matters are received in a much more sensitive manner (including the above [i.e., differences of opinion]).

Among the advisable and prudent manners of behavior that will ameliorate the situation: to refrain from debates and arguments (by changing the discussion to another matter), to positively affect her in an oblique and non-threatening manner, and the like.

Obviously you are to conduct yourself in keeping with the law stated in *Shulchan Aruch Admur HaZakein*, the conclusion of laws of *Ona'ah* [where the Alter Rebbe states that women are to be treated with tenderness since they have a more sensitive nature]. Also [it is important that you] give her credit for her accomplishments.

This is in addition to that which we have previously spoken about providing her with encouragement [regarding her activities] so that she finds satisfaction and is blessed with success [in her efforts].

(*Kuntres Tzaddik L'Melech*, Vol. VII, p. 242)

A HUSBAND SHOULD BE READY TO FOREGO MATERIAL MATTERS IN ORDER TO ACHIEVE SHALOM BAYIS

In reply to your letter of Teves 28 in which you write about the state of the relationship between you and your wife [and that she has moved out of the house]:

It is known to what extent our Sages, of blessed memory, speak glowingly about the importance of *Shalom Bayis* and that "When husband and wife merit, the Divine Presence resides in their midst." [7] Thus, it is necessary for you to see that many of your wife's friends speak to her and convince her to return home.

7. *Sotah* 17a.

From now on may peace reside in your home, thus causing joy to reside there as well.

You will surely take to heart the statement of our Sages, of blessed memory, that women are of a more emotional nature ("*Nashim da'atan kalah*")[8] and "their tears flow more easily"[9] [i.e., they have a more sensitive nature], and "the gates of tears are never closed."[10]

Therefore, in many situations such as that which you are facing, the husband should sacrifice material matters as much as he can. This is particularly true in your situation, where it is important to bear in mind the effect your relationship has upon your children.

Bearing in mind the importance of all the above, surely after giving the matter due thought and consideration you will find the means to bring about *Shalom Bayis* in actuality.

May G-d grant you success in your endeavor.

(*Igros Kodesh,* Vol. VIII, p. 211)

ACHIEVING SHALOM BAYIS BY MEANS OF KINDLINESS AND AFFABILITY

I preface my letter by asking your pardon [for the remarks that follow] and noting that which is already known, that "Great is peace, for which reason the entire Torah was given," as the *Rambam* rules at the conclusion of the Laws of Chanukah. Moreover, this is also clearly stated in a *Mishnah*,[11] [that peace is] "the vessel that holds and sustains G-d's blessing."

---

8. *Shabbos* 33b; *Kiddushin* 80b.
9. *Bava Metzia* 59a. See also *Shulchan Aruch Admur HaZakein*, conclusion of laws of *Ona'ah*.
10. *Berachos* 32b.
11. Conclusion of *Uktzin*.

[In light of the above,] permit me to prompt you to act with alacrity with regard to strengthening the state of *Shalom Bayis* in your home.

I refer quite simply to an improvement in the conditions of *Shalom Bayis* that exist between you and your wife *tichye*.

I write this in light of what I was able to discern "between the lines," as well as "between the lines" of the conversations I had with your wife and her frame of mind when she was here.

It would be beneficial for you to be very yielding in your personal feelings and exert as great an effort as possible in this area [of achieving proper *Shalom Bayis*].

The proof of the importance of achieving *Shalom Bayis* is well known, known as well in the revealed portion of Torah, in that G-d states that it is a *mitzvah* to erase His Divine and Ineffable Name, a name written specifically by a *Kohen* and with specific sacred intent, as long as it leads to peace between husband and his wife.

This is so even when the wife has conducted herself, Heaven forfend, in a manner necessitating "accusation" (*kinui*).

Surely then, achieving *Shalom Bayis* is crucial when we are speaking of a modest and morally upstanding wife [an *isha tzanu'ah*] who has trained and educated her family in the path of *Chassidus*. Any and all effort to achieve *Shalom Bayis* is a tremendously great and exalted *mitzvah*.

It is my hope that you will cause me joy by conveying to me glad tidings that you are endeavoring with all your ability to bring about *Shalom Bayis*, doing so in a manner that is consonant with the statement of our Sages, of blessed memory, that women are of a more emotional nature ("*Nashim da'atan kalah*").[12]

---

12. *Shabbos* 33b; *Kiddushin* 80b.

You should therefore cause your wife's heart to rejoice in an appropriate manner. By this I mean, that your attitude and behavior towards her should not be with testiness and irritability (*ongetzoigenkeit*), but with kindliness and affability (*hasboras panim*).

Surely even the above few lines will suffice [to rouse you in your efforts to achieve *Shalom Bayis*]. I await glad tidings [with regard to the above].

(*Igros Kodesh*, Vol. XII, p. 301)

THE PURSUIT OF MANY MITZVOS AND GOOD DEEDS DOES NOT ACT AS AN IMPEDIMENT TO SHALOM BAYIS

... With regard to the matter at hand:

G-d granted the Jewish people 613 *mitzvos*. Our Sages came along and stated that each and every individual is to endeavor to perform these commandments above and beyond the letter of the law. Then along came *Toras HaChassidus* and elucidated that all *mitzvos* are to be performed with fervor and vitality.

[Although all the above is demanded of us,] nevertheless it is patently obvious that there exists no contradiction between one *mitzvah* and the next, or between one *mitzvah* and all the others. On the contrary, "One *mitzvah* brings about another."[13]

So, too, with regard to your question that keeps on repeating itself in many of your letters [concerning the prioritization of your time and activities]:

All those activities that you mention: your sacred work of bringing others in your environs to Torah and its *mitzvos*, your sacred work in ... , your assistance in the home — and "Great is peace between husband and wife," as our Sages note that this brings about that the Divine Presence to reside among them — all are necessary and extremely noteworthy.

---

13. *Avos* 4:2.

Since G-d, "Who fashions the hearts of them all,"[14] placed upon you all the above at one and the same time, you surely possess the capacity to arrange your life in a manner that not only will these activities not contradict one another, but that one will actually assist the other.

You, yourself, after all, write in your letter that your wife was pleased that you successfully influenced a certain young man, causing him to become a G-d-fearing individual.

[Your wife derived this pleasure] notwithstanding the fact that she surely realizes that her being pleased with this will no doubt cause you to act with even more vigor and desire in this area of your activities. Clearly then, your wife is satisfied with these activities and enthusiastically agrees that they continue.

Understandably, when one is at a distance — in fact, even when one is in close proximity — it is impossible to state unequivocally that from a certain hour to a certain hour you should engage in this activity and then, until a certain hour you should engage in a second activity, etc. For it all depends on the conditions of the place, day, mood, the pressing nature of events, etc., etc.

On the other hand, "The Torah was not given to angels,"[15] [and when the Torah demands something of us, we have the capacity to perform it]. Therefore do not exaggerate the difficulty in ordering your affairs in a manner that your activities come together and complement each other.

(*Igros Kodesh,* Vol. XI, p. 98)

---

14. *Tehillim* 33:15.
15. *Berachos* 25b.

WHEN SHALOM BAYIS PROBLEMS RESULT FROM A HUSBAND'S LACK OF KOACH GAVRA

Our Sages, of blessed memory, speak — in the Torah of *Truth* — in wondrous terms about the greatness of marriage and its permanence.

With regard to all matters that depend on the subconscious, it often happens that quite unconsciously and sometimes without even any noticeable actions [on the part of the individual], changes occur, and as a matter of course, the "blocks," etc., disappear.

You should therefore continue the course of action that has demonstrated benefit and success (at least [continue this course of action] for a period of time): Which is to say, [continue with] visitations to the psychologist, etc., and [continue] visiting the Holy Land during vacation periods.

Moreover — and this is of great import: *Minimize* worrying about the above, and be as inattentive and heedless as you possibly can (*le'hasiach da'as*) to this entire problem.

May G-d bless you with success and may you be able to convey glad tidings [with regard to the above].

(From a handwritten response of the Rebbe)[16]

16. Printed in *Kfar Chabad* Magazine (together with a facsimile of the Rebbe's holy handwritten response), Issue 834.

Chapter Five

Problems of Shalom Bayis During the Early Years of Marriage

Problems of Shalom Bayis Soon After the Wedding

To each of them *sheyichyu:*[1]

All the problematic matters about which you write occur very often in the early days of many marriages (until the newly married couple gets used to and comfortable with each other). These problems then diminish until they completely cease to exist, as long as *both parties* make a good faith effort [to work out their problems].

Moreover — and this is of greatest import: All the above difficulties are absolutely incomparable to the vital importance of *Shalom Bayis*, for as our Sages instruct us, "When a husband and wife are meritorious, the Divine Presence dwells in their midst."[2]

When you will contemplate and act in accordance with the above, you will *surely* see an immediate improvement in the situation — and it will continue to improve and become better, and together you will merit many long and goodly days and years.

In order to hasten the improvement of the situation and to make it easier, etc., it would be advisable that in addition to your talking and working it out between yourselves, you should

---

1. The couple wrote to the Rebbe several weeks after their wedding, about a number of serious problems regarding their marriage. So serious, in fact, were these problems that they were not sure whether to continue their marriage.
2. *Sotah* 17a.

also choose someone from your family or a rabbi who is a friend of the two of you (or possibly to use all of the above), and they should together with you discuss and deliberate where you should live, the details about the manner of earning a living, etc.

(From a response of the Rebbe, printed in *Likkutei Sichos*, Vol. XXIV, p. 466)

HUSBAND AND WIFE ADJUST TO EACH OTHER THROUGH MAKING ALLOWANCES FOR THE OTHER

... On the question of how to achieve an easier adjustment in the family life of husband and wife: Firstly, it should be remembered that it indeed occurs very frequently that such an adjustment is required, inasmuch as there are two people involved [in a marriage, individuals] who come from two different families, etc.

It should also be remembered that there is no such thing as human perfection and that one person must make allowances for the other, in the same way that one expects the other to make such allowances.

(From a letter of the Rebbe, written in the year 5733)

PROBLEMS OF SHALOM BAYIS DURING THE FIRST FEW YEARS OF MARRIAGE

I am in receipt of your letter in which you write about the situation in your household with regard to *Shalom Bayis*.

Experience teaches us that when problems of *Shalom Bayis* arise during the first few years of marriage, the best way to mutually resolve the problem and attain a state of peace — for many long years together, to the mutual satisfaction and contentment of both parties — is by not being overly attentive and sensitive to issues that cause disagreement. Surely, the matter in dispute is but a temporary issue; the less attention paid to it the better.

At the same time, each of you should place emphasis on those goodly matters concerning which you are in mutual harmony and agreement. The more you act in the above manner, the quicker the *Shalom Bayis* matter will resolve itself and straighten out.

It is self-understood that I on my part will try to do what I can — in an appropriately tactful manner — to help ameliorate the situation. However, I do hope that you, on your part, will act in accordance to that which I wrote above.

In addition to the above, there is the well-known verse,[3] "As water mirrors the face to the face" [i.e., just as the nature of water is to reflect an image], "so does the heart of man to man" [i.e., so, too, is it in man's nature to mirror the emotion of another]. This is particularly true regarding the mirrored and reflective emotions of husband and wife.

Moreover, our Sages tell us that, "a woman's tears flow relatively easily,"[4] [i.e., they have a more sensitive nature]. Thus, your demeanor and your comportment with regard to your wife should be mild-mannered, agreeable and pleasant.

May G-d grant you success, so that in the immediate future you are able to notify me about a mutual change for the better. May you both together raise your son *sheyichye* to Torah, *chuppah* and good deeds.

(*Igros Kodesh,* Vol. XIV, p. 62)

DO NOT ALLOW POTENTIAL FUTURE PROBLEMS TO AFFECT PRESENT SHALOM BAYIS

... Your concern that you and your wife have dissimilar opinions regarding the education of your children is something that will first come to play after the two of you will be blessed

---

3. *Mishlei* 27:19.
4. *Bava Metzia* 59a. See also *Shulchan Aruch Admur HaZakein*, conclusion of laws of *Ona'ah*.

with children and they will reach school age — a matter that will take place *many* years from now.

Until then, it is an absolute verity that [at that time] *each of you* will form opinions that are quite different from the opinions that you presently hold. Additionally, it is unquestionable that the arrival of children brings about a *great* deal of closeness between their parents.

One cannot know beforehand the substance of the change [in opinion and attitude towards the child's education,] as well as the great degree of nearness [that will ensue in the future, especially through becoming parents to children].

According to our faith, we are to have *immense* hope that all the above [positive transformations] will transpire in ample measure.

In terms of actual practice and conduct, you should see to it that the two of you reconcile, and may you witness the fulfillment of G-d's blessing that your marriage be an "eternal edifice."

In conclusion — it is patently clear that there is to be a strengthening and enhancement of your *Shalom Bayis*, inasmuch as each and every Jew is to strengthen and enhance those aspects that he shares in common with all other Jews. How much more so with regard to husband and wife.

[Follow these positive steps,] rather than delving and concentrating on those matters where the two of you do not see eye-to-eye — regarding something that may come to pass after many years.

(From a letter of the Rebbe, printed in *Likkutei Sichos*, Vol. XXIV, p. 467)

CHAPTER SIX

Shalom Bayis Problems and Means of Resolution

SHALOM BAYIS IS OF PRIMARY IMPORTANCE — NOT WHO IS RIGHT AND WHO IS WRONG

... I trust it is unnecessary to emphasize to you at length that the Jewish way of life, together with its customs, etc., is not only very significant in its generalities, but is also significant in all its details and in the very order and arrangement of matters.

In light of this, it is obvious how truly important are peace and harmony between a husband and wife, since the *mitzvah* of making peace between a husband and wife is counted among the *mitzvos* whose fruits a Jew enjoys in this world, while the "principal" remains for the World to Come.[1]

These are mentioned right at the beginning of the *Siddur* — together with the morning blessings, which are recited even before starting the actual morning prayers.

With this in mind, it will prove somewhat easier to understand that even if one party were to be completely in the right (or almost completely in the right), while the other party were to be completely in the wrong (or almost completely in the wrong), it would still be incumbent upon both parties to do everything in their power to restore peace and harmony.

Certainly this duty becomes paramount in the case of a husband and wife who hold prominent positions in the

1. *Peah* 1:1.

community, as a result of which other Jews look up to them for example and guidance.

Clearly, an outsider cannot know, nor can he be told, what compelling reasons there might be for such a situation. The outsider can only observe and draw his own conclusions, since he will not inquire about, nor is it possible to inform him of, all the factors and extenuating circumstances, should there be any. Add to this the fact that it concerns a couple, both of whom are active in the sphere of Jewish education.

Moreover, and of course this is also most essential, G-d has blessed you with children, good children, who require the attention, love and upbringing of both parents. These children are surely entitled to receive what is due them from their parents.

Beyond a shadow of doubt, each of you must do everything possible not to further strain your relationship, but on the contrary, the two of you must endeavor to strengthen your relationship, restoring it to its full unity and harmony.

As to the situation itself, namely, who is right and who is wrong, I cannot, of course, go into this, nor is it necessary in light of what has been said above. For the important thing, as already stated, is to strengthen your family ties, this being the overriding consideration.

However, it would be well if the two of you could find a mutual friend before whom both of you could unburden yourselves in a frank exchange of grievances.

It is possible that an outsider, who at the same time is a friend, might see more objectively and find the best way to straighten things out, and [moreover, do so] as soon as possible, so that once again peace and harmony may reign in your home.

Hoping to hear good news from you,

(From a letter of the Rebbe, written in the year 5730)

GO ALL OUT TO ACHIEVE SHALOM BAYIS

In reply to your letter of the 16th of Kislev:

According to the adjudication of our Rabbis, of blessed memory, concerning the greatness of peace between husband and wife, it is understood that you must try to do whatever you can in order to achieve *Shalom Bayis* [with your husband]. This is particularly so, as this also has an impact on the happiness of your daughter and your grandchildren *sheyichyu*.

The Torah commands us [to achieve *Shalom Bayis*], especially as stressed in *Toras HaChassidus* and in particular in the well-known *Sichah* of my father-in-law, the Rebbe, where he states:[2]

Man was created with both a right and left eye. Looking with the "right eye" means looking in a favorable manner — when looking upon a Jew one must look with one's "right eye" to see his fineness and goodness, etc.

Since we were so commanded in our Torah, the Torah of Life, we have surely been granted the power and ability to perform this command. And "There is nothing that stands in the way of one's will."[3]

(*Igros Kodesh*, Vol. XX, p. 66)

ACHIEVING SHALOM BAYIS BY LOOKING AT ONE'S SPOUSE WITH THE "RIGHT" EYE

... In light of the ruling of our Sages, of blessed memory, about the greatness of peace between husband and wife, it is understandable that as much as possible you should attempt to achieve *Shalom Bayis*, particularly so since achieving *Shalom Bayis* will also provide happiness and contentment to your daughter and your grandchildren *sheyichyu*.

---

2. *Sefer HaSichos 5691*, p. 158.
3. See *Zohar*, Vol. II, p. 162b.

We have been commanded in our Torah — especially as stressed in *Toras HaChassidus* and in the well-known *Sichah*[4] of my father-in-law, the Rebbe — that man was created with a right eye and a left eye. The right eye, i.e., looking at an individual in a "right" and positive manner, teaches us that we are to view [all] our fellow Jews [and how much more so our spouses] with kindness and benevolence, etc.

Since this has been commanded us by our Torah, the Torah of Life, surely we have been granted the power and capacity to properly perform this commandment. And "There is nothing that can stand in the way of one's will."[5]

(*Igros Kodesh,* Vol. XX, p. 66)

Achieving Shalom Bayis Entails a Readiness Of Both Parties to Compromise

... Furthermore (and of greatest import, and it has a bearing on earning one's livelihood as well):

It is imperative for the *Shalom Bayis* between you and your wife to markedly improve. It is therefore necessary that both you and your wife each give in and compromises a bit: do not insist on "winning" and "vanquishing" the other, and being "right," (*v'loi likoneis l'natzchonus*) and the like.

(From a letter of the Rebbe, printed in *Heichal Menachem* III, p. 189)

It Takes Two to Battle

... By and large in matters such as these [i.e., strife and arguments leading to a lack of *Shalom Bayis*], as well as with regard to conflicts — strife and war in general — there must be the active participation of both parties.

4. *Likkutei Dibburim*, Vol. IV, p. 1,412 (*Sefer HaSichos 5691*, p. 158).
5. Cf. *Zohar,* Vol. II, p. 162b.

Thus, when one of the parties realizes that the other party is not taking the conflict to heart, neither being emotionally pulled in nor taking part in the arguments, then little by little, the fierce emotions and the desire for an argument and fight will ebb and ultimately completely fade away.

In your case as well, it is imperative that you contain your emotions and not enter into arguments.

Bearing in mind that women are of a more emotional nature ("*Nashim da'atan kalah*")[6] and "their tears flow more easily"[7] [i.e., they have a more sensitive nature], you should forego those matters that are possible to do without and do not take the remaining matters to heart. As a result, the "good side" will ultimately emerge victorious.

(*Igros Kodesh*, Vol. VIII, p. 58)

AN INDIRECT APPROACH IS MORE EFFICACIOUS IN REESTABLISHING SHALOM BAYIS

... It is well known that with regard to familial matters between husband and wife, an oblique approach rather than a direct approach is more efficacious, as is verily observed.

Another point: an indirect approach minimizes the points of disagreement and arguments [between the couple], and if the possibility but exists to gloss over these differences, or at least to diminish them, so much the better.

This [non-accusatory and non-threatening approach] is very effective [in achieving *Shalom Bayis*] as it draws the couple closer together. For as the verse states, "As water mirrors the face to the face so does the heart of man to man."[8] This reflective approach

---

6. *Shabbos* 33b; *Kiddushin* 80b.
7. *Bava Metzia* 59a. See also *Shulchan Aruch Admur HaZakein*, conclusion of laws of *Ona'ah*.
8. *Mishlei* 27:20.

[whereby tenderness begets tenderness,] is the natural inclination of each and every human being.

May it be G-d's will that the couple merit the [fulfillment of] the saying of our Sages, of blessed memory, that "When a husband and wife are meritorious, the Divine Presence dwells in their midst."[9]

(*Igros Kodesh,* Vol. XVIII, p. 373)

ACHIEVING SHALOM BAYIS SHOULD NOT BE REGARDED AS NECESSITATING "INCONVENIENCE" OR "SELF-SACRIFICE"

Your letter reached me with some delay.

Although it is difficult to reply in detail to the issues you raised through the medium of a letter, I will, at any rate, answer briefly:

1) Concerning the establishment of a close relationship between two people, especially between spouses, which clearly is one of the most important aspects of human life, especially in the view of our Torah — the Creator, in His infinite kindness, has revealed and given to us certain directives and precepts.

The purpose of these directives and precepts is, on the one hand [i.e., on the positive side], to ensure the conditions under which the couple will be blessed with an abundance of blessings, and on the other hand [i.e., on the preventative side], to guide and protect them from undesirable acts and consequences.

In light of the above, it makes no sense to postpone the [good] things that have to be carried out, nor [does it make sense] to postpone those matters that should not be done, on the assumption that in the end the proper form of conduct will ensue in a measured manner. For, obviously, the Divine blessings are needed immediately in daily life, as is the [need for the] prevention of undesirable consequences.

---

9. *Sotah* 17a.

2) The above would be valid even in a case where the said factors are presumed but not proven, inasmuch as there is so much at stake, while the effort would in fact involve only a certain inconvenience on the part of those who do not yet appreciate the importance of these matters.

Actually, there can be no question about the validity of this approach in the present case, where the Jewish way of life has been tested and proved over the course of thousands of years.

Moreover, Jewish history has shown that those who adhered to the Jewish way of life, in accordance with the will of G-d, have been able to surmount all difficulties and to survive in the face of great odds, whereas those who chose to deviate from this way of life, even temporarily, suffered serious consequences.

3) Where there is a real desire, and a real feeling for one another, and a real quest for a harmonious life together, one clearly does not allow any inconvenience to get in the way of such important goals that have so great a bearing on one's life.

Such inconveniences will not be considered a "sacrifice"; on the contrary, the good attained through this effort is all the more laudatory, bringing people closer together.

On the other hand, it is too much to expect of a person who believes honestly and sincerely in these Divine laws and precepts that he or she will compromise on such fundamental issues.

I trust that, without entering more deeply into all the aspects of the situation, the above comments will suffice, for they have a clear bearing on the matter of which you write.

May G-d grant you the strength to disregard any difficulties and to order your daily life in accordance with the directives and imperatives of our Torah.

And if there really are any problems or any inconveniences involved — of what significance can they be in relation to the inner peace and inner harmony that a Jew attains when he follows in the way of his ancestors, and identifies himself with his great spiritual heritage.

(From a letter of the Rebbe, written in the year 5732)

PROBLEMS REGARDING SHALOM BAYIS CONNECTED WITH MAJOR CHANGES IN THE COUPLE'S LIFE

In reply to your letter in which you touch upon all that has transpired from the time you married until the present. You write about the effect this has had upon you, to the extent ... [that you are ready to divorce your husband]:

After reading your letter with due deliberation, my considered opinion is that notwithstanding all the untoward events that have occurred, they do not *in any way* serve as grounds to destroy, G-d forbid, a Jewish home [and marriage] — whose purpose is, as stated in the text of the marriage blessings, to be "an eternal edifice."

This is particularly so, as the [untoward] events transpired during the time that you were in the midst of a major move — not only in the physical sense but also in the spiritual sense. For the move from being single to being married and from *Eretz Yisrael* to the Diaspora, etc., entails major changes.

[The crucial importance of achieving *Shalom Bayis* and staying married] is especially understood when considering the great importance of peace in general and *Shalom Bayis* in particular, to the extent that G-d decrees that His Name be erased by [placing it in] water so that peace can be brought about between husband and wife.[10]

You should submit your contentions to a local *Rav* who adjudicates on a regular basis. Understandably you should do this in the presence of your husband, so that the *Rav* will be able to

10. See *Makkos* 11a, and sources cited there; *Rambam*, conclusion of *Hilchos Chanukah*.

hear both sides of the story as related both by you and your husband in each other's presence, which is crucial in ascertaining the truth.

If the two of you but desire, you can surely find many ways of improving and enhancing your relationship with each other. This [necessary effort to achieve *Shalom Bayis*] is in keeping with the many directives and statements of our Sages.

Included in the above is the statement we make on a daily basis at the beginning of each day, that [achieving peace between husband and wife is among those matters that one] "enjoys the fruits in this world, while the principal reward comes in the World to Come."

I hope that you will give due consideration to the above words — few in number [but great in import]; moreover, that you contemplate these words in a manner consistent with the seriousness and importance of the matter [i.e., keeping your marriage intact]. May G-d grant you success.

With blessings for glad tidings with regard to all the above.

(*Igros Kodesh,* Vol. XVIII, p. 225)

PROBLEMS REGARDING SHALOM BAYIS CONNECTED WITH FINANCIAL DIFFICULTIES

When, with G-d's help, your husband's financial situation will improve, his mood will surely improve as a matter of course. Both of you will then become less sensitive and the disagreements and bickering will evaporate.

In the interim, you on your part should make an effort not to pay attention at all [to your husband's ill temper and moods]. This as well will serve to dissipate the disagreements and bickering.

[As to your question about the advisability] of accepting a part-time job — it is a sound idea.

(From a written response of the Rebbe, from the year 5731)

PROBLEMS REGARDING SHALOM BAYIS CONNECTED WITH DIFFERENCES IN DEGREE OF OBSERVANCE

... You write about your problem in regard to your relationship with your wife, having been married to her for fourteen years and having been blessed with children. You also indicate that the problem is connected with the observance of the Jewish way of life.

In the latter point lies the answer to your questions:

It is the Jewish way of life that dictates, in accordance with the Torah, that having been married for a number of years and having been blessed with children who are to be brought up to a life of Torah, *chuppah* and good deeds, it is imperative to do everything possible to preserve the peace and unity of the family to the fullest extent.

At the same time, it is also clear that inasmuch as the Torah is the Jew's very life, there can be no sacrificing of it even in the hope of preserving the family; for a peaceful and harmonious Jewish family life is possible only if it is based on the observance of the Torah and *mitzvos*, the very same principle being found in reference to the Torah, "Its ways are ways of pleasantness, and all its paths are peace."[11]

Needless to say, while it is necessary to insist upon the Jewish way of life, this should be conveyed to your wife in a pleasant way, taking her feelings into account, and not giving the impression that there is any desire to "boss" her around or to show her who is the master of the house.

Rather, it should be explained that this is really for the benefit not only of both the parents and the children, but also, no less important, of the entire Jewish people, since the family unit is the very basis of our Jewish people as a whole.

---

11. *Mishlei* 3:17.

It is a matter of common experience, arising out of human nature, that when two people are involved in a personal disagreement, it is hard for them to discuss their differences dispassionately, and one or the other, or both, may get drawn into a heated debate where things are said which would otherwise not have been said.

Therefore it is customary in such a situation for the matter to be brought before an Orthodox rabbi, one who is experienced in these matters and also bound to treat such matters in strict confidence. Thus, the whole business may be discussed fully and openly in the presence of the rabbi, and hopefully straightened out in accordance with his guidance.

I would like to add one important point, which is that a Jew who accepts the Jewish way of life in his daily life, even where this is not spontaneous but has come about through the influence or even persuasion of another, sooner or later he will come to realize the truth.

The truth of the matter is, that all this was for his ultimate benefit, and whatever his original feelings might have been — even if he was reluctant or resentful, he will certainly be most grateful for being so influenced, as this has set him on the path of truth and true happiness.

(From a letter of the Rebbe, written in the year 5735)

WHO IS TO MAKE CONCESSIONS IN MATTERS OF RELIGIOUS OBSERVANCE

I am in receipt of your letter, in which you write about your background and also about the change in your way of life, since you were raised in an environment which was not one hundred percent Orthodox; however, in due course you underwent a change and became more observant of the Jewish way of life, and this has created friction between you and your husband.

I can well understand that your husband, who has not gone along with you on this path, or at any rate, has lagged behind, may sometimes be somewhat dissatisfied that his partner in life has made greater progress, while he has not yet found the strength to follow suit. On the other hand, in such a case it is clear who has to make concessions in order to avoid friction.

It is in fact easier for the non-religious person to make the concession, inasmuch as this does not involve any transgression or sin [on his or her part], or even any strong conviction or burden of conscience; at the very most it might involve certain inconveniences.

On the other hand, for the religious person, a concession means a breach of strong religious feelings and of convictions that go to the very core of the soul.

From the above it follows that your spouse will eventually change his attitude, especially if you follow the ways of the Torah, which are ways of pleasantness and peace.

The above holds true as long as your spouse perceives that there is no attempt by the other party to be domineering, but that the other party is motivated only by strong feelings and the conviction of having found the truth, and consequently want to see a near and dear person share in this new-found truth.

May G-d grant that all the difficulties and friction will soon disappear, and that you and your husband may mutually go along the path of truth, the way of the Torah and *mitzvos*, with joy and gladness of heart.

May you together bring up your children to a life of Torah, *chuppah*, and good deeds, in good health and ample sustenance.

(From a letter of the Rebbe, written in the year 5725)

DIFFICULTIES OF SHALOM BAYIS ARE OFTEN LESS PROBLEMATIC THAN FIRST IMAGINED

... I was unhappy to note — as indicated by the content of your letter — that your *bitachon* in G-d, something that is expected from every Jewish daughter and particularly from a Chassidic woman, is somewhat lacking. Inevitably, this has an effect on your health and on your household.

Every Jewish man and woman must constantly remember that just as G-d conducts the world as a whole — the macrocosm, so, too, does He conduct the microcosm that is each and every one of us.

Just as G-d has a say in the world as a whole, so does He surely have a say in the microcosmic world of each individual. We are to rely on Him, realizing that He surely directs all matters in a positive and goodly direction.

This [positive direction] should not be impeded by evincing a lack of *bitachon* in blessed G-d, nor by matters that are not in accordance with the Torah, one of which is the lack of proper *Shalom Bayis*.

Until after the arrival of *Mashiach*, there exists no individual who can possibly be perfect — devoid of all flaws. Thus, beyond a shadow of a doubt, just as the one person is flawed, so too is the other.

Just as we have no desire to have our own flaws revealed and pointed out, so too should we not emphasize and magnify the faults of others. The above holds true with regard to all Jews; how much more so with regard to husband and wife.

My purpose here is not to admonish you, but to make you aware that the situation is not as harsh and problematic as you imagine. Moreover, your situation is not as uncommon as you think.

Each of you should gloss over certain [negative] matters, for surely you would do better to [concentrate on and] find those ways that lead to enhanced *Shalom Bayis*.

When *Shalom Bayis* reigns, it serves as the receptacle into which G-d pours His blessings and success, accompanied by good health, ample sustenance, and *nachas* from children.

(*Igros Kodesh,* Vol. V, p. 61)

Problems of Shalom Bayis Are Often a Consequence Of Difficulties Regarding Earning a Livelihood

In reply to your letter in which you describe the [negative] state of the relationship, etc.:

Unfortunately, yours is not an exception; a similar situation exists in tens and tens of homes.

Experience has shown that the best way to ameliorate the situation is by *not* placing undue emphasis on this, and surely not to exacerbate the situation with sharp and cutting remarks.

Producing this positive change of behavior within oneself is easier than one imagines, as one sees how this positive manner of behavior leads in a very short time to goodly and beneficial results.

This is particularly so, since in very many instances, the true and inner reason for negativity and dismal moods and attitudes towards the other spouse stems from difficulties or stress with regard to earning a living.

It is human nature that at times such as these, the stress is expressed to a greater extent within the relationship that one has with those with whom one is close, rather than with those who are more distant or even strangers. Indeed, there are very few exceptions to this manner of conduct.

When you ponder and consider well the goodness that G-d has granted you in the past few years, true and persisting goodness, this will strengthen your trust and assuredness that G-d will surely continue to shower you with kindness and goodness.

You yourself will then come to the realization how small and inconsequential were these unpleasant chance incidents in comparison to the many kindnesses that G-d has shown you.

(*Igros Kodesh*, Vol. XIV, p. 42)

DO EVERYTHING POSSIBLE TO ACHIEVE SHALOM BAYIS

It saddened me greatly to hear that the misunderstanding between your son *sheyichye* and his wife *tichye* has yet to straighten itself out. I am even more upset to hear that they are still living apart and that there are even those who speak of the possibility that they will divorce.

As you surely are able to influence your son, I therefore find it obligatory to write to you that you must realize that we are dealing here with a matter that will affect your son throughout his *entire life*. Thus, for you as well — as his parents — this matter is a *life issue*.

You must throw yourself into this matter and see to it that *Shalom Bayis* exist between your son and his wife, so that they construct a normal family life. They should live their lives independently, neither with her parents nor with his parents. This will make it easier for them to strengthen their *Shalom Bayis*, living their lives in a manner that is appropriate for a Jewish family.

I have heard about the various reasons that are offered as the cause of the difficulty in reestablishing *Shalom Bayis*. I have also heard the reasons your son related to me when he was here.

However, after all these reasons, I feel obligated to point out that we are dealing here with a life-matter relating to two young people. It is thus forbidden to mix other issues into this matter.

We must also remember that which our sacred Torah teaches us: G-d says that in certain circumstance His Sacred Name may be erased so long as it is done in order to establish *Shalom Bayis* between husband and wife.

This itself leads us to understand how great is the danger to all who place obstacles in the path of *Shalom Bayis* and how tremendously great is the reward for those who assist in reestablishing the *Shalom Bayis* between husband and wife.

I surmise that since you are parents who desire the happiness of your children, I need not elaborate further regarding this matter. I trust that you will do everything possible to reunite your son with his wife and rebuild their *Shalom Bayis*.

May G-d help you that as a result of your efforts, you be blessed with good health and *Yiddishe nachas* from these children as well as from your other children.

(*Igros Kodesh,* Vol. V, p. 433)

WHEN LACK OF SHALOM BAYIS IS A RESULT OF GOSSIP AND SLANDER

... According to your description of the present state of your relationship with your second wife, and after having set forth all your complaints and all that transpired in your arguments, I am of the opinion that all the above lacks sufficient grounds and is merely a conflict of words.

Surely among the causes [of your difficulties with regard to *Shalom Bayis*] are that certain other individuals are meddling as well as spreading *lashon hara* [slanderous gossip] and the like.

Accordingly, it is my considered opinion you that should seek various means and approaches to bring about a rekindling of affection between you and your wife.

If at all possible, it would be best that you move your place of residence, so that you are not together with those whom one may suspect are spreading gossip and exaggerations. After that, one may look forward to a gradual warming of the relationship and a diminution of disharmony, until ultimately peace and tranquility will reign in your midst.

Understandably, in keeping with the saying of our Sages, of blessed memory, that "a women's tears flow more easily"[12] [i.e., they have a more sensitive nature], your words should be soft and gentle and will thus be more readily received.

[When you active in the above manner, you will perceive how] "And a soft response subdues anger"[13] — even when there are grounds for the anger, and particularly in this instance when there are no real grounds, merely hurt feelings that resulted from mere utterance of words.

[Moreover,] our Sages, of blessed memory, have stated[14] that "a second marriage is in accordance to one's deeds."

Aside from the simple meaning, one may infer from this that in a second marriage the relationship depends on one's actions to a much greater extent than in a first marriage — since the second marriage is primarily according to one's deeds.

(*Igros Kodesh,* Vol. III, p. 438)

PRIESTLY EFFORTS TO ACHIEVE SHALOM BAYIS

In reply to your letter of the 19th of MarCheshvan: I was astonished to read that you are angry (*bi'kepeida*) at your wife. Although our Sages, of blessed memory, do state that *Kohanim* tend to be irritable (*kapdanim*),[15] [nevertheless, this should not be so in the present situation]:

---

12. *Bava Metzia* 59a. See also *Shulchan Aruch Admur HaZakein*, conclusion of laws of *Ona'ah*.
13. *Mishlei* 15:1.
14. *Sotah* 2a.
15. See *Bava Basra* 160b.

Firstly, you need not embark on your service as a *Kohen* with this trait — there are so many [*Kohanic*] matters that take precedence. Additionally, this matter of irritability with others is out of place. Why use this trait with regard to another, when a person is closest to himself [and if you need be irritated, then be irritated at your own faults]?

This is particularly so when your ire has been aroused not regarding a stranger but regarding [your wife], the one individual who makes you complete and who transforms you from "it is not good [for man to be alone...]" into ["one who finds a wife, finds] good."

Possibly, you still remember what I related to you concerning an individual [who was having problems with *Shalom Bayis*], at which time I mentioned that the state of one's *Shalom Bayis* has an impact on one's sustenance, as in the *Mishnah*, conclusion of [tractate] *Uktzin* and in *Likkutei Torah*, conclusion of the section of *Berachah*.

If it is necessary — according to the Torah — to make an effort via natural means to earn a livelihood, surely one must be diligent in those matters [such as *Shalom Bayis*] which, according to the Torah has an effect on one's earning a living. It surely is unnecessary to go on at greater length about a matter that is so obvious.

I merely want to draw your attention to the fact that with regard to matters such as these, [i.e., controlling one's temper, becoming irritable, etc.,] although people consider them trivial and picayune, it is specifically such matters that are the true test as to what extent an individual is truly a *chassid* — as is to be understood from many holy *Sichos*.

May it be G-d's will that in the immediate future you inform me that you have begun [not merely to make a perfunctory effort in this direction, but rather that you have begun] *working* on yourself in this area, at which time you will [see that you will] also merit [that you will be able] to inform me that your efforts are meeting with success.

(*Igros Kodesh*, Vol. XII, p. 87)

BASELESS LOVE AS REMEDY FOR SHALOM BAYIS EVEN WHEN THERE ARE LEGITIMATE COMPLAINTS

I received your letter dated Sunday, *Parshas Behaaloscha*, in which you describe the situation in your household — that this is your second marriage (your first marriage ended in divorce) and that the state of *Shalom Bayis* is not as it should be.

You do not write in detail about the divorce of your first wife, whether she also desired it or was forced into it. If it was the latter and you do not know where she is presently to ask her personal forgiveness, then you should assemble a quorum of men and ask her forgiveness before them.

Other things to do to enhance your *Shalom Bayis*: Check the *mezuzos* in your home. Act with forbearance to the greatest degree possible.

Also known are the sayings of our Sages that women are of a more emotional nature ("*Nashim da'atan kalah*")[16] and "their tears flow more easily"[17] [i.e., they have a more sensitive nature], and "Is it not sufficient that they save you from sin?"[18] and particularly since they raise your children.

Additionally, you write that your son learns in a *yeshivah* of Lubavitch — surely your wife has a share in this, for as you

---

16. *Shabbos* 33b; *Kiddushin* 80b.
17. *Bava Metzia* 59a. See also *Shulchan Aruch Admur HaZakein*, conclusion of laws of *Ona'ah*.
18. See *Yevamos* 63a.

yourself write: she has always assisted you, etc. Moreover, "a second marriage is in accordance with one's deeds." [19]

When you will act in this manner, it is hoped that your *Shalom Bayis* situation will improve and you will be able to convey glad tidings in this regard.

You should observe [the custom of] reciting Psalms (at least as it is divided according to the days of the month) each day following morning prayers — any addition to this is to be lauded. You should also study each day the daily section of the weekly Torah portion together with the commentary of *Rashi*.

Also, find friends who will influence your wife and children so that everyone will become closer to one another.

Even if — according to what you write — you have many legitimate complaints about your wife, one must always remember that the present exile resulted from the sin of baseless hatred.[20] Consequently, the rectification of this matter is through baseless love.

That is to say, that we are to love a person even when this love is not at all warranted, and not even warranted according to the Torah. Nonetheless, [baseless] love of one's fellow is required commensurate with the degree of baseless hatred — the reason why "we were exiled from our land and driven far away from our soil."[21]

When each and every individual in your environs will conduct himself in this manner, this will have a corresponding effect on his portion in the world. And when the entire Jewish nation shall conduct themselves in this manner, this will refine the entire world, thereby drawing down the immediate revelation of *Mashiach*, as explained in chapter 37 of *Tanya*, see there.

---

19. *Sotah* 2a.
20. *Yoma* 9b.
21. Text of the *Mussaf Amidah* for the Festivals.

You surely give *tzedakah* at least on Mondays and Thursdays. It would be appropriate for you to do so on a daily basis prior to the *Shacharis* prayer, (except, of course, on *Shabbos* and *Yom Tov*).

(*Igros Kodesh,* Vol. VI, p. 143)

A MARRIAGE THAT RECEIVED A REBBE'S BLESSING FACILITATES SHALOM BAYIS

In reply to your letter of Sunday, *Parshas Pekudei,* in which you notify me that there is a lack of *Shalom Bayis* between you and your wife, and you ask my advice as to what you should do:

Since my father-in-law, the Rebbe, blessed your marriage with a blessing of *mazel tov*, and the words of *tzaddikim* are eternal, you should therefore appease your wife and explain to her the above.

Surely, if there be a need, the elders of *Anash* will assist you in establishing a state of peace between the two of you.

Through calm words and acts that will draw you closer to each other, you will surely find the path to her heart and there will be peace and tranquility in your domicile, and the two of you will be blessed with healthy and viable children.

(*Igros Kodesh,* Vol. XXI, p. 121)

It pained me to hear that — for the time being — there is a lack of *Shalom Bayis* in your home. I hope that what I heard is not true, or at least only a short-lived situation. Please write to me about this (in whatever language is most convenient for you).

In any event, I wish to remind you that the Rebbe, my father-in-law, of blessed memory, blessed your marriage with your husband with a blessing of *mazel tov*. You and your husband must therefore serve as fit receptacles to receive this blessing; you should have a warm Chassidic home blessed with healthy and viable children.

(*Igros Kodesh,* Vol. XXI, p. 122)

SHALOM BAYIS IS ACCOMPLISHED BY CONCESSIONS MADE BY THAT INDIVIDUAL FOR WHOM CONCESSION IS BUT AN INCONVENIENCE, NOT A MATTER OF PRINCIPLE

In reply to your letter of the 4th of Sivan, in which the two of you write about the problems that have developed between you as a result of differences regarding your beliefs in [the authenticity of] the Torah and its commandments; [the husband believing in the authenticity of the Torah and its *mitzvos* and the wife claiming that she does not].

Moreover, [you write that] these difficulties are particularly severe, to the extent that they have affected the state of your *Shalom Bayis*:

(a) It is important to bear in mind that in such a situation, when a religious and believing individual is forced not to perform *mitzvos*, then this has a strong effect on his conscience as he is forced to act against his beliefs and religion.

On the other hand, when a person who is — according to her thinking — not religious and not a believer and nonetheless performs *mitzvos*, it does not go against her conscience and principles — it merely involves inconvenience and the like. For example, this may cause her to refrain from eating non-kosher food; however, there are so many kosher foods that she is able to eat, among them delicacies, etc.

Shalom Bayis is one of the most lofty and important ideals — particularly when husband and wife have been blessed with children. For it is obvious how important it is for the children to grow up in a home where peace reigns, and to grow up in a whole home, a home where there is both a father and mother.

Therefore, it is patently obvious that even when it is necessary — to use the familiar expression — to forego important matters, and surely when it merely involves foregoing conveniences, that this be willingly done in order to establish *Shalom Bayis*, and particularly for the sake of the children.

Moreover, this is to be done with joy and gladness of heart, not with a feeling that a supreme sacrifice is being made under pressure, etc. Rather, the feeling is one that they are doing yet another good thing for the sake of the home and for the benefit of the children, in addition to it being for the benefit of the parents themselves.

The conclusion from the above points is clear and simple. It is my hope that at the earliest possible opportunity, the wife — who thinks she does not believe — will forego her comfort and do all she can to establish *Shalom Bayis* — moreover, [not only to establish *Shalom Bayis,* but] to strengthen the *Shalom Bayis* [that has been established], and to do so, as stated above, with joy and gladness of heart.

With blessings for glad tidings with regard to all the above — and the sooner the better.

P.S. Understandably, I must make my position known regarding your [i.e., the wife's] writing that you are not a believer.

I will preface my remarks by stating that human beings possess the ability and free choice to change their deeds, speech and thoughts. However, people are incapable of changing their essence.

The essence of each and every member of the Jewish people — the heritage of all generations [of Jewry] — is belief in the G-d of Israel, a simple and total belief.

[This belief] defines, affects and is the soul of the entire individual, affecting all his limbs and organs, although — as mentioned above — the Creator of man desired to provide him with free choice to conduct himself with regard to his deeds and speech in a manner that either is or is not consonant with his essence.

We understand from the above that ultimately the essence and foremost aspect [of the individual] triumphs over the [superficial] layers that conceal the essence, layers that result from [deficient] education, [inappropriate] environment, or many, many other external factors.

(*Nitzutzei Or*, p. 98)

Chapter Seven

The Role and Non-Role of Rabbis, Friends and Relatives In Achieving Shalom Bayis

The Rebbe and Rebbetzin — Paving the Way

Once, while a certain *chassid* traveled past the Rebbe's home, he noticed the Rebbe and Rebbetzin entering a vehicle. His interest aroused, he followed the vehicle until he saw the Rebbe and Rebbetzin enter a certain Park Avenue apartment.

The next day he returned to the address and discovered which apartment the Rebbe and Rebbetzin had entered.

Upon politely inquiring from the apartment dwellers as to the purpose of the visit of the Rebbe and Rebbetzin, he ascertained the following:

The couple was not aware who the Rebbe and Rebbetzin were. However, they had been having *Shalom Bayis* problems.

The previous day, they related, some Rabbi and his wife visited them, had a cup of tea with them and spoke to them about ways in which they could rectify their *Shalom Bayis* situation. As a result of that visit, their *Shalom Bayis* situation had vastly improved.

(As printed in a *Teshurah*)

Using the Good Offices of a Third Party

In reply to your letters from *Rosh Chodesh* and the 5th of Sivan:

It pained me to read that the relationship and *Shalom Bayis* between you and your husband has yet to improve. As is well known, even the most fragile peace is better than the most minor and trifling quarrel. And it is self-understood that a sturdy peace is even better.

After all you write in your letters, I still do not see anything substantial that should serve as a cause for the antagonism between you and your husband. I therefore retain my opinion, which I stated to you previously when you visited with me, [that the two of you should try to work matters out].

However, if you feel that the situation is too difficult for you and your husband to work out on your own and the present situation is intolerable, then possibly the two of you should follow your husband, the *Rav's*, suggestion — although with slight modification:

The two of you should set forth your grievances before one or two individuals who are mutual friends of yourself and your husband.

At times, someone who is at a distance [from the issues] can, [by being more objective,] more clearly illuminate the situation. He can suggest a strategy how to resolve the state of affairs, although those who are intimately caught up in the dispute have failed to notice this approach because of their anger and subjective involvement.

May G-d abundantly bless your home and provide ample *Shalom Bayis*; may you be able to rapidly notify me of glad tidings with regard to the above.

(*Igros Kodesh,* Vol. IX, p. 100)

WHEN THERE ARE PROBLEMS OF SHALOM BAYIS SPEAK FACE TO FACE WITH A RAV

... With regard to the relationship between you and your wife and the problems of *Shalom Bayis*:

Understandably, this is dependent on very many factors that are absent in your letter [to me] — and [understandably so, for] it is impossible to list them all in a letter.

Generally, according to the dictates of our Torah, the Torah of Life, in such instances one should speak *face to face* with a local *Rav* who adjudicates on a regular basis — and it would be best that this *Rav* be from your community. He will impart to you the Torah ruling.

(*Likkutei Sichos*, Vol. XIX, p. 514)

WHEN THERE ARE PROBLEMS OF SHALOM BAYIS BOTH PARTIES SHOULD AIR THEM OUT WITH THE LOCAL RAV

... It is customary among Jews that when the *Shalom Bayis* between husband and wife needs to be strengthened and is in need of improvement, both parties air their grievances before the communal *Rav* or the *Rav* of the area, and then follow his directive — a directive that is in keeping with the opinion of our Torah, the Torah of Life.

It is self-understood that both sides — both the husband and the wife — must demonstrate good will and make a good faith effort to strengthen the peace.

"Peace is the vessel that holds and sustains G-d's blessing"[1] for all one's needs, and "There is nothing that stands in the way of one's will."[2]

In light of the above, it is self-understood that you should conduct yourself according to the custom of fine and upstanding Jewish women — each of whom is called "*Akeres HaBayis*,"[3] the mainstay and foundation of the home — both with regard to the

1. *Mishnah*, conclusion of *Uktzin*.
2. See *Zohar*, Vol. II, p. 162b.
3. See *Bereishis Rabbah* 71:1; *Zohar*, Vol. I, p. 154a.

observance of the commandments in general, and particularly those commandments that depend on the Jewish woman.

It would be proper for you to check the *mezuzos* in your home if they have not been checked during the past twelve months. You surely are aware of and observe the fine custom[4] of giving some money to *tzedakah* prior to candle lighting on the eve of every *Shabbos* and *Yom Tov*.

Among the guidance and counsel given to increase one's measure of security in G-d [that everything will turn out for the best] — if indeed there is a need for this sense of reassurance — is to recite the 23rd Psalm in the Book of *Tehillim*, i.e., the Psalm: "G-d is my shepherd; I shall lack nothing.... "

With my blessing that G-d fulfill the desires of your heart for the good, and that you be able to convey to me glad tidings.

(*Igros Kodesh*, Vol. XXV, p. 135)

How a Third Party Should Go About Strengthening a Couple's Shalom Bayis

In reply to your letter from Sunday, which because of its important content I hasten to answer, without waiting for its turn:

In it you write about the relations and interactions between husbands and wives, etc.

In keeping with the directive of our Sages, of blessed memory,[5] about the reward for bringing peace between husband and wife, that one "enjoys the fruits [in this world, while the principal reward comes in the World to Come"], it is simple to understand that any and all efforts and attempts [at achieving *Shalom Bayis*] are worthwhile.

It is also clear that in matters such as these it is impossible to provide hard and fast rules, for it depends on the personality of

4. *Kitzur Shulchan Aruch*, 75:2. See also *Kaf HaChayim*, 263:34.

5. *Shabbos* 127a.

the husband and wife, as well as the nature of the environs in which they find themselves and in which they live.

However, it is also certain that each and every individual can indeed be approached and [constructively] affected.

[This can be accomplished] when the person ponders and seeks the proper manner by which he can affect this particular individual [whom he is trying to positively affect in his *Shalom Bayis*] — approaching him time and again in a pleasant manner, but with firmness and with words that emanate from the heart.

All the above is not difficult to convey in a heartfelt manner, for this is of tremendous importance to both husband and wife, as well as to all future generations that will emanate from them.

That which is beneficial in all such instances [of trying to reestablish *Shalom Bayis*] is conducting oneself in the manner of Aharon, the "Lover of Peace," as described in the 12th chapter of *Avos d'Rebbe Nassan*.[6]

May G-d bless you with success in [your efforts to] help create a proper house in Israel, and that it be grounded in Torah and *mitzvos* even as it is practiced on a consistent daily basis. ...

If the careers of the above mentioned couple permit, there is room to say that their traveling together for a few weeks to a vacation spot and the like for a second honeymoon, would rectify the entire situation.

(*Igros Kodesh,* Vol. XX, p. 19)

FRIENDS CAN ASSIST A COUPLE IN REBUILDING SHALOM BAYIS

In response to your letter of *Rosh Chodesh* Nissan, in which you write about your family situation, etc., [i.e., problems with regard to *Shalom Bayis*]:

---

6. Aharon would go to each of the individuals involved in the dispute and relate that the other person desires to reconcile.

Generally, when seeking to enhance the relationship between husband and wife, the best and most appropriate way, [when the wife is disgruntled by some aspect of the marriage,] is to have friends speak to her.

It would be appropriate that her women friends in particular speak to her, inasmuch as they are capable of influencing her — in a pleasant and agreeable manner — to conduct her home (together with her husband) in a goodly manner, both materially and spiritually.

In keeping with the verse[7] "Stones are worn away by [the relentless flow of] water," so, too, when these friends will speak to her time and time again, particularly when their words will be heartfelt, then eventually they will succeed [in changing her attitude and bringing about *Shalom Bayis*].

It goes without saying that you on your part are to conduct yourself [vis-à-vis your wife] in a manner of friendship and peace.

The combination of all the above will hasten *Shalom Bayis* in your home.

May G-d bless you that you and your wife together succeed in raising all your children *sheyichyu* to "Torah, *chuppah,* and good deeds," in a serene frame of mind and with ample sustenance.

(*Igros Kodesh,* Vol. VIII, p. 342)

FRIENDS CAN MORE READILY BRING ABOUT SHALOM BAYIS THAN RELATIVES

You write about your sister and the family situation, [i.e., the poor state of *Shalom Bayis*] in her home:

We verily observe that in such situations, the words of friends and associates [of the couple] can have a greater effect [in bringing about *Shalom Bayis*] than the words of relatives.

---

7. *Iyov* 14:19.

Understandably, this should be done in a manner that it not be known [by your sister and her husband] that the request [for mediation and intervention of friends] comes from you.

It is self-understood as well that your sister should not be overly critical, even with regard to those matters in which she feels she is one hundred percent in the right.

Since "Great is peace" and especially *Shalom Bayis*, "peace in the home," it is worthwhile to restrain your emotions and contain yourself, as long as this will strengthen the peace.

I surely need not mention that your sister should be even more scrupulous in observing the rules and regulations of *Taharas Hamishpachah* ((*niddah*, *hefsek taharah*, immersion in a kosher *mikveh*, etc.), as unlawful closeness [between husband and wife] leads to distance [between them].

It is my hope that you will find the appropriate language by which to explain the above to your sister. ...

(*Igros Kodesh*, Vol. XVIII, p. 119)

AT TIMES ADJUSTING TO EACH OTHER IS BEST ACCOMPLISHED VIA AN UNDERSTANDING AND FRIENDLY THIRD PARTY

To the two of them:[8]

1) Our Sages, of blessed memory, state that man and wife (who are married in accordance to the Torah and Jewish law) merit to have the Divine Presence reside in their midst.

2) This is particularly so, since the husband is a *Kohen* and G-d has blessed [the two of] you with children.

3) Our Sages, of blessed memory, state that G-d's residing [in their midst] obliges and necessitates peace — true peace — in that site.

---

8. The following is a written response of the Rebbe to a couple who were having problems with *Shalom Bayis*. They traveled from overseas for the specific purpose of receiving the Rebbe's advice and blessing.

4) Our Sages, of blessed memory, [further] state that no two people think alike, for which reason it may well become necessary that from time to time there must be consultation and mediation through the good offices of discerning friends (*yedidim mevinim*) [who can objectively advise them].

5) It is best when these [discerning friends] are *Rabbanim* — individuals who are knowledgeable of the view of Torah.

6) Therefore, upon your return to your city, get in touch with a rabbi in your city, relate to him my response, and ask him for his directives.

7) Surely (afterwards) you will both speak with him, and may G-d grant you success.

8) Check the *mezuzos* and *tefillin*.

9) I will mention you in prayer for glad tidings, on the holy resting site of my father-in-law, the Rebbe.

10) With blessings that you celebrate the Festival of Shavuos and the Receiving of the Torah, in a joyful and internalized manner.

(From a handwritten response of the Rebbe, printed in a *Teshurah*)

HOW GROWN CHILDREN CAN ASSIST THEIR PARENTS IN ACHIEVING SHALOM BAYIS

In reply to your letter, the content of which is [your informing me about] the [torturous] relationship between your father and mother *sheyichyu*:

In matters such as these it is self-understood that your mother *tichye* should not get drawn into quarrels, even regarding those matters regarding which she feels her husband is entirely in the wrong. When your father will see that your mother has no desire to quarrel and clash, his desire to bicker and squabble will weaken and continuously lessen with time.

You should also have your mother ask friends in the community to influence your father to improve his attitude. Understandably, your father is not to know that your mother asked them to influence him [that he change for the better].

Since all matters require aid and assistance from Above, it would be appropriate for your mother to give every weekday morning some coins to *tzedakah,* in addition to her surely conducting herself in the custom of Jewish women to give *tzedakah* prior to lighting candles on the eve of every *Shabbos* and *Yom Tov.*

It is self-understood that all the above is in addition to the brothers and sisters *sheyichyu* influencing — in an honorable and gentle manner — their parents that father and mother improve their mutual relationship.

(*Igros Kodesh,* Vol. XVIII, p. 169)

WHEN A COUPLE IS HAVING SHALOM BAYIS PROBLEMS THOSE WHO ARE CLOSEST TO ONE OF THE PARTIES SHOULD REFRAIN FROM MIXING IN

... I find particularly alarming that which you write that your sister, [who is having *Shalom Bayis* problems,] is presently staying in her parents' home.

To our sorrow, we have clearly seen the disastrous results that can occur when other individuals mix into the affairs that should be strictly between husband and wife. This is the case even if those who intervene are very close to them.

(At times the intervention of those who are very close to one of the parties can more easily lead to damage than to healing. For inasmuch as they are so very close to one of the spouses, they [may very well instinctively and subjectively] side with that party. This [lack of objectivity] would not be the case when a total stranger intervenes.)

(*Igros Kodesh,* Vol. X, p. 58)

EVEN VERY CLOSE RELATIVES SHOULD NOT MEDDLE WHEN THERE IS AN ISSUE BETWEEN HUSBAND AND WIFE

In reply to your letter from ... in which you notify me about the [*Shalom Bayis*] situation that has arisen between your sister [and her husband,] your brother-in-law, and their dispute:

For some time now I have viewed with extreme disfavor the practice of some individuals who meddle and intrude when there is an issue between husband and wife. Even those who are [the] closest [of relatives], such as a brother and sister or father and mother, do not help matters by interfering.

Moreover, it is known how our Sages, of blessed memory, have spoken at length regarding the great import of peace between husband and wife, to the extent that G-d decrees that His Name be erased by [placing it in] water so that peace can be brought about between husband and wife.[9]

When a peripheral individual mixes in — and surely that individual possesses not only a divine soul [whose intent is surely solely to help] but also an animal soul [whose motives may well be questionable] — then by and large this does not help bring about *Shalom Bayis*.

I do not desire to address this matter at greater length because I am not sure that my words will be efficacious. Conversely, if they will help, then the above words surely suffice.

And in response to your question with regard to the actual dispute: "There is justice in Israel," and the disputants need to clarify the law by *Rabbonei Anash*.

May G-d bless His nation with peace.

(*Igros Kodesh*, Vol. V, p. 289)

---

9. See *Makkos* 11a, and sources cited there; *Rambam*, conclusion of *Hilchos Chanukah*.

NON-INTERFERENCE BY ONE SIDE OF THE FAMILY MAY WELL LEAD TO NON-INTERFERENCE BY THE OTHER SIDE

You ask for my advice [regarding the *Shalom Bayis* difficulties between your daughter and her husband].

In the situation you describe, it would be better not to interfere in the state of affairs that has arisen between your daughter and her husband *sheyichyu*. This will enable them to ultimately work things out between themselves.

Even if the interference of others [from the other side] cannot be avoided, it is still better that you do not do so. By refraining from interfering, they too will cease to meddle, as they will see that the other side is not mixing in.

Possibly it will not be easy for you to refrain from interfering. Nonetheless, when you consider the benefit [of your restraint] for your daughter, you will probably be able to accomplish this.

(*Igros Kodesh,* Vol. XIV, p. 465)

CHAPTER EIGHT

Spiritual Assistance and Hindrances to Shalom Bayis

"SHALOM BAYIS" BETWEEN BODY AND SOUL IMMEASURABLY ENHANCES ACTUAL SHALOM BAYIS

... It is self-understood that when I will be on the holy resting place of my father-in-law, the Rebbe, I will mention Mr. ... and his wife for a blessing of *Shalom Bayis*.

We need remember though that which is most essential: it is imperative that there exist in them "*Shalom Bayis*" between soul and body [i.e., the spiritual "husband and wife"]. This immeasurably enhances and makes it easier for *Shalom Bayis* to reign in their home.

(*Igros Kodesh*, Vol. V, p. 225)

PROBLEMS OF SHALOM BAYIS ARE AVOIDED WHEN THE HOME IS ESTABLISHED ON PROPER TORAH FOUNDATIONS

You mention in your letter the problems of *Shalom Bayis* that exist in the home of Mr. and Mrs. ...

It must be explained to the father that which I had already written to him when the *shidduch* was still under discussion, that the couple must establish their home on proper Torah foundations. This is of vital importance not only to their spiritual well-being and happiness, but to their physical well-being and happiness as well. Truly this is so, and whether they understand it or not makes very little difference.

For it is similar to following the directives of an esteemed physician. One benefits thereby even when one does not know why the doctor has so ordered. How much more so, when it is a command of the Creator of the world, who is also the Healer of all flesh.

(*Igros Kodesh,* Vol. V, p. 224)

Marriage at Its Most Wholesome Is Achieved Through Strict Observance of Taharas Hamishpachah

... So that the shared intimate life may be entirely wholesome, it is necessary to strictly observe the laws and regulations of *Taharas Hamishpachah.*

For although these laws require separation for a certain period of time, this distancing has the effect of bringing the couple closer together in the time that follows. However, closeness during the time when separation is mandated results in separateness when there *should* be closeness.

Thus, in the majority of cases, true harmony and peace in married life are directly related to the observance of the laws and regulations of *Taharas Hamishpachah.*

(From a letter of the Rebbe, written in the year 5733)

The Positive Effects of Scrupulous Observance of Taharas Hamishpachah on Shalom Bayis

In reply to your letter about Mrs. ... *tichye*, who does not have *Shalom Bayis*, and the blame is being placed on her mother-in-law's frequent taxing and aggravating visits to their home, etc.:

It is almost certain that this [*Shalom Bayis* problem] is because there are matters of *Taharas Hamishpachah* [laws of family purity] that are in need of rectification. For in addition to all other untoward matters that result from a lack of scrupulous observance of *Taharas Hamishpachah*, the above [difficulty of *Shalom Bayis*] is included as well.

This is in keeping with the statement of our Sages (*Niddah* 31b) that the laws of *Taharas Hamishpachah* were given in order for the wife to be beloved to her husband as on the day of their marriage. [It thus follows that a lack of observance of these laws leads to a lack of love between husband and wife — problems of *Shalom Bayis*.] Understandably, this is in addition to the effects [that a lack of observance of these laws has] on the children, etc., etc.

It is my hope that you will find the right words to explain to her parents all that was stated above. Experience has taught us that the less discomfited one is [in transmitting these matters and laws,] the more all parties are satisfied in the end — although, as is self-understood, it must be transmitted in a gentle manner.

(*Igros Kodesh*, Vol. IX, p. 302)

LACK OF PROPER OBSERVANCE OF FAMILY PURITY MUST BE RECTIFIED TO REPAIR DAMAGE IN SHALOM BAYIS

It would seem that your conduct with regard to *Taharas Hamishpachah* has been improper, and as a result, damage has accrued to the two of you.

Hopefully, you will come to this realization (through having others explain this to you — and [better yet,] possibly on your own).

Thus you will both realize that this alone [i.e., your lack of proper conduct with regard to *Taharas Hamishpachah*] is the sole reason for the change of feelings towards each other. Separation and the like is [therefore] not the answer [and the proper resolution of your difficulties].

You are to rectify and repent for your misdeeds — and [bear in mind that] one cannot flee from G-d. Rather, you must from now on particularly act with precisely correct conduct as regards your married life....

(From a handwritten response of the Rebbe)[1]

1. Printed in *Beis Moshiach* Magazine (together with a facsimile of the Rebbe's holy handwritten response), Issue 287.

VERY OFTEN PROBLEMS OF SHALOM BAYIS ARE A RESULT OF IMPROPER CONDUCT REGARDING LAWS OF FAMILY PURITY

In reply to your letter from *Erev Shabbos Kodesh* in which you ask for a blessing and offer a *Pidyon Nefesh* for your sister *tichye* [who is having problems with *Shalom Bayis*]:

At an auspicious time I shall read the *Pidyon Nefesh* at the holy resting place of my father-in-law, the Rebbe. May G-d will it that just as you were the one who made the request [for a blessing that the *Shalom Bayis* situation improve], so too may you be able to convey glad tidings with regard to the above [i.e., that the *Shalom Bayis* situation has improved].

You will surely forgive me for the lines that follow, but I feel obliged to note that very often the lack of peace — especially between a Jewish husband and wife — comes as a result of closeness that is improper according to our Torah, the Torah of Life.

This is in keeping with the phrase,[2] "Your evil shall castigate you," i.e., that the [iniquitous] conduct itself serves as chastisement, by clearly demonstrating that the consequences of such behavior are entirely opposite of that which was hoped for and expected.

Understandably, it is difficult for me to go on at length about such a matter, particularly with regard to people whom I don't know personally. Nevertheless, as stated above, I find it obligatory to underscore the above.

This is especially so, since it is quite possible that the matter that requires rectification stems from a lack of knowledge [of the pertinent laws], or the matter requiring rectification may be of Rabbinic origin and not an explicit Torah prohibition. It is self-understood, though, that in reality this is not an excuse, since

---

2. *Yirmeyahu* 2:19.

"The words of the Rabbis are even 'sweeter' than the words of the [written] Torah."[3]

Since all matters should also be accomplished by way of natural means, therefore, in light of the fact that all human beings are capable of being influenced by others, it would be appropriate to find an individual who is capable of influencing them with regard to the Above [i.e., with regard to strengthening their observance of the laws of family purity].

[Moreover, the chances of success in influencing them to strengthen their observance and thereby enhancing their *Shalom Bayis* is considerable,] for it is known that in matters such as these special assistance is granted from Above, since this [matter of bringing about *Shalom Bayis*] is among those matters that one "enjoys the fruits in this world, while the principal reward comes in the World to Come...."[4]

(*Igros Kodesh,* Vol. XVIII, p. 235)

PROBLEMS OF SHALOM BAYIS MAY WELL BE THE RESULT OF IMPROPER CLOSENESS

... You write about the situation regarding *Shalom Bayis*, etc., that it is in need of improvement:

In many instances this comes as a result of improper closeness (which is to say, [a closeness] that is not permitted according to our Torah, the Torah of Life).

Repentance, however, is efficacious — complete regret for past behavior and proper resolutions for the future, and actually behaving in a manner consonant with those resolutions.

(*Igros Kodesh,* Vol. XX, p. 108)

---

3. See *Avodah Zarah* 35a and the commentary of *Rashi* on the words, "*Divrei Dodecha.*" See also *Eruvin* 21b.
4. *Shabbos* 127a.

... In quite a few instances, situations such as these [i.e., problems with *Shalom Bayis*] result from improper closeness — [closeness] during those times that this closeness is not permitted according to our Torah, the Torah of Life.

Since at times this may be the result of an incomplete knowledge of all the laws [relating to *Taharas Hamishpachah*], therefore you and your husband should clarify these laws from a rabbi who regularly adjudicates matters of Jewish law.

You should do so with the intent of conducting yourself in the proper manner from here on. And "There is nothing that stands in the way of one's will."[5]

It would also be appropriate that you check the *mezuzos* in your residence, that they be fit according to Jewish law, and that you observe the fine custom of upstanding Jewish daughters — that of giving *tzedakah* prior to candle lighting on the eve of every *Shabbos* and *Yom Tov*.

(*Igros Kodesh*, Vol. XXIV, p. 117)

CHECK THE MEZUZOS

I received your letter dated Kislev 17, with the attached *Pidyon Nefesh* for Mrs. ... for [improved] *Shalom Bayis*. When I will be at the holy resting site of my father-in-law, the Rebbe, I will pray for her for the above.

You do not write any details about her. I therefore hope that she is conducting a Jewish home, and I merely wish to encourage her that at the earliest possible opportunity she checks the *mezuzos* in her residence, and that prior to candle lighting on the eve of every *Shabbos* and *Yom Tov* she give charity to the *Tzedakah* of *Rabbi Meir Baal HaNes*.

[Their *Shalom Bayis* will be enhanced] in particular, when they will come to the realization and resolution that at times one

5. See *Zohar*, Vol. II, p. 162b.

must acquiesce [to the desires of the other]. This minimal action can accomplish very much.

She will then speedily be able to relay glad tidings that the *Shalom Bayis* situation is improving.

(*Igros Kodesh,* Vol. V, p. 81)

POSSIBLE SPIRITUAL REASONS FOR DIFFICULTY IN SHALOM BAYIS AND SPIRITUAL METHODS FOR AMELIORATING THE SITUATION

In reply to your letter ... in which you write that you are a mother to six children and that there is strife in the household; also, quite often the health of your family is not as it should be, etc.:

In situations such as these, it is necessary to first and foremost be *scrupulous* and *meticulous* in the observance of the *mitzvah* of *Taharas Hamishpachah* (*niddah*, the days of *hefsek* and *taharah*; a kosher *mikveh*, and the like).

The *mezuzos* in the home should be checked to assure that they are all kosher, and your husband should check his *tefillin*. You should give some coins to *tzedakah* prior to candle lighting on the eve of every *Shabbos* and *Yom Tov*, and your husband should similarly give *tzedakah* at least on Mondays and Thursdays, prior to prayer.

The two of you should also verify whether your *shidduch* with each other did not wound the pride of any Jewish young man or woman (that is to say, that either of you were engaged to someone else and then pulled out of the *shidduch*).

(*Igros Kodesh,* Vol. X, p. 110)

CHAPTER NINE

Remaining Married

THE VITAL NEED OF CONTINUING A MARRIAGE FOR THE SAKE OF THE CHILDREN

To begin with: you married according to "the laws of Moshe and Israel" with the recitation of the *Sheva Berachos*, the Seven Nuptial Blessings, with the utterance of and in G-d's name.

G-d has blessed you with children (the greatest blessing that can accrue to a Jewish couple).

Consistent with the above, G-d placed upon you (and your husband *sheyichye*) one of the greatest *mitzvos*, that of rearing, training and educating your children, and ultimately to lead them to the *chuppah*, to marriage. Moreover, this is to be done in the best manner possible, i.e., by the two of you together — as a *complete* [and unbroken] family unit.

As mentioned above, this is your genuine good fortune and happiness (in this world as well as in the World to Come), as well as your mission [in life, as you stand as an example] before your friends, and indeed, before all Jewish women.

It is therefore impossible for you to feel happy and fulfilled (or even to feel at peace) if you were to — G-d forbid — divorce your husband.

After all your children *sheyichyu* have married, then there may be a point as to whether you should give this matter, [i.e., divorce,] further thought or not.

Since this is a command of our holy Torah — [a command of] G-d — surely this [manner of conduct will lead to] your true happiness and contentment.

(From a handwritten response of the Rebbe)[1]

DIVORCE ONLY AS THE ABSOLUTELY LAST RESORT EVEN WHEN SPOUSE IS NOT LIVING A TORAH LIFE

In reply to your letter from the end of the month of Tammuz — which was slightly delayed in transit — in which you write about the state of affairs with regard to your family life and your relationship with your wife *tichye* [that it is in need of improvement]:

There is the well-known teaching of our Sages, of blessed memory,[2] regarding [the relationship with] "the wife of one's youth," as the verse states,[3] "Can one possibly despise the wife of his youth?!" This is particularly so when G-d has blessed the two of you with children who are being educated in the path of Torah and *mitzvos*.

In light of all the above, it is understandable how the thought of divorce, G-d forbid, is totally unacceptable. For a divorce is only a final measure after having exhausted all efforts to bring about *Shalom Bayis*. This approach [that a divorce is to be avoided if at all possible] is consonant with the directives of our Torah, a Torah of Life and a Torah of Peace.

According to the description in your letter, it would seem that you have a strong influence on your wife. However, until now — seemingly because you have been so busy running your business and the like — you have not given the matter proper attention.

---

1. Printed in *Beis Moshiach* Magazine (together with a facsimile of the Rebbe's holy handwritten response), Issue 81.
2. See *Sanhedrin* 22a.
3. *Yeshayahu* 54:6.

At the very least, you did not [properly] occupy yourself in this matter, i.e., after having given due consideration and thought to the best way to accomplish an improvement in *Shalom Bayis*. This is why up until now you have not been all that successful.

Accordingly, all attempts and efforts [at enhancing your *Shalom Bayis*] are advisable [and should be pursued]. Particularly, since by doing so you will draw your wife incrementally closer as well [to Judaism] and you will connect her to a life that is lived in accordance with Torah.

This incremental change for the better will have a profound effect on her, since this will have been accomplished not only in order that you do not divorce, but that she intellectually accept living her life in a religious manner.

It is understood that there are special situations where according to the Torah, divorce is inevitable, Heaven forfend. But all this comes to play only after there is incontrovertible evidence that the situation [is hopeless and] cannot be changed for the better.

When you will write to me your and your mother's name as well as your wife's and her mother's name, as well as the names of the children, I will mention them for a blessing at the holy resting site of my father-in-law, the Rebbe.

It would be appropriate that on a daily basis after your morning prayers, you should follow the directive of reciting a portion of Psalms, as they are divided into the days of the month. Also, give some coins to charity prior to your prayers every weekday.

(*Igros Kodesh,* Vol. XV, p. 358)

AVOID DIVORCE EVEN WHEN HUSBAND HAS COMMITTED GRIEVOUS SIN

... I do not know if until then you will conquer your evil inclination and its blandishments, [the evil inclination] not being satisfied with the [goodly] state of affairs [of peace between husband and wife, which results in] the "Divine Presence resides in their midst," as affirmed by our Sages, of blessed memory.[4]

It [i.e., the evil inclination] desires, G-d forbid, to take away your contentment and prevent you, G-d forbid, from continuing together with your husband to build an eternal edifice with blessed generations of children and grandchildren.

... G-d has provided you with all matters of *good* in this regard, and the choice is up to you whether you will perceive this goodness, or whether you will accept the wiles and urgings of the evil inclination who says that [what is indeed] good is in fact evil [and what is evil is in fact good].

... For the commission of one sin [by your husband] (even as great a sin as that which you have mentioned) does not justify [your] committing a different transgression, or failing to perform a *mitzvah*.

... I will mention you in prayer at the holy resting site of my father-in-law, the Rebbe, that you make a proper and good resolution, particularly now [as we find ourselves in the month of Elul,] when "the King is in the field," etc.

(From a letter of the Rebbe, printed in *Likkutei Sichos*, Vol. XXIV, p. 468.)

THE POWER TO WITHSTAND THE TEST OF OVERCOMING THE PERCEIVED NEED FOR A DIVORCE[5]

If G-d presents an individual with a great test (and our Sages, of blessed memory, have stated[6] that G-d only asks of individuals that which they are capable of accomplishing), it is an indication

---

4. *Sotah* 17a.
5. The present letter is a continuation of the Rebbe's previous letter. It would seem that the wife responded to the Rebbe that under the circumstances it was a very great test for her not to divorce her husband — perhaps too great a test.
6. See *Shemos Rabbah* 34:1; *Bamidbar Rabbah* 12:3.

that He has previously already provided mighty powers [to that individual] to withstand the test.

... I do not compel or oblige (anyone in general, and you in particular) to accept my opinions, suggestions and explanations — I only respond with my view concerning those matters which I am asked.

Clearly, the decision in this matter (with regard to your continuing the marriage ... etc.) depends entirely on you...

(From a letter of the Rebbe, printed in *Likkutei Sichos*, Vol. XXIV, p. 468.)

DO NOT CONSIDER DIVORCE AS THE ONLY OPTION

In reply to your letter from the 11th of Av, in which you write about the course of events that led to your *shidduch*, the [poor] relations that currently exist between you and your husband, and that during an argument it was decided to approach the Jewish Superior Court (*Beis Din Elyon*), etc. [in order to obtain a divorce].

You conclude your letter with the statement that you are currently at war with your husband as well as with his entire family.

You of course understand that it is extremely difficult to offer an opinion based on the claims of but one side. For the axiom, "A person is too close to his own self [to be entirely objective],"[7] applies to even the most sterling individual.

Since the two of you have decided to approach the *Beis Din Elyon* — surely you are referring to practiced and qualified Rabbis — there will be ample opportunity to have both sides heard and also to hear their opinions, opinions of individuals who have no [subjective] side in this matter.

7. *Yevamos* 25b; *Sanhedrin* 9b.

However, that which I hasten to note with regard to what you wrote, is the following:

a) The statement that "you are currently at war with your husband as well as with his entire family": There are sufficient grounds [in this statement] to say that you are [not only at war with them, but] also at war with yourself.

For [a good and decent] family life is a matter that is at the very core of a person's life and existence, and any hasty and incorrect step can have disastrous results for both husband and wife. Moreover, quite often they [i.e., these not well thought out and incorrect steps] have an even greater negative effect on the party that took these steps than on the other party.

It is self-understood that in no way am I intending here to offer an opinion as to the problem itself or as to how it may be solved. For as I have stated earlier, I have heard only one side of the argument.

I merely want to express my concern with regard to the impression I received [from your letter] that you are trying to exacerbate the relationship between the two of you, so that the matter may reach a clarification and resolution at the earliest possible opportunity. However, not always is a clarification in such matters either good or beneficial.

b) Possibly the following is even more crucial — and that is with regard to that which you write that you are approaching the *Beis Din* for the purpose of obtaining a divorce:

You seem to imply that this is the only option that you find feasible, and I believe that you, too, would conclude that this is indeed your position, [i.e., that you maintain that divorce is the only option].

However, an impartial outsider can judge much more objectively than those who are utterly involved in the matter [whether divorce is indeed the only option]. Therefore, it is improper to decide beforehand that you are approaching the *Beis Din* with an inflexible objective, [i.e., the objective of obtaining a divorce].

What astounded and perplexed me about your actions and the steps you are taking is the fact that although you are religious and you have received a religious education, etc., and your general outlook on life is a religious one, nevertheless you acted on this matter in a contrary manner — with the intent to end the relationship between you and your husband.

Surely I need not explain to you that conduct in keeping with the directives of our Torah, the Torah of Life, is not one of using it as a bargaining chip or for applying pressure. Rather, it has its own value system, fundamental to the relationship between man and his Creator, the Conductor of his life.

Adjusting our personal behavior to the directives of [Torah and] the Giver of the Torah, draws down blessings of the Giver of the Torah on those who conduct themselves in this manner.

Included in these blessing are levelheaded deliberation and consideration; correct appraisal and evaluation of the situation that the person presently finds himself in; [and the ability to make] proper resolutions that will lead to his true good fortune and happiness.

Thus the text of supplication for our personal needs in our thrice-daily-recited *Amidah* begins with the petition that G-d "graciously bestow upon us wisdom, understanding and knowledge."

From the positive you can infer the negative — weakness in the ties that bind man to his Creator by acting in a contrary manner, hinders in achieving all the above; it deprives the person of something that is crucial and vital at all times, and particularly during those times in a person's life when he desires to solve intricate and critical problems.

I am sending you this letter via "express" and [I have answered this letter] before I answered other letters that were received before yours, with the hope that the above few lines in comparison to the importance of the subject, will rouse you to reflect on this matter once again and change your view, in light of the three points mentioned above.

Most important is that your actions be in consonance with the directives of our Torah, the Torah of Life.

I would be delighted to receive confirmation from you that my hopes [that you have changed your views] have been realized.

(*Igros Kodesh,* Vol. XIV, p. 96)

AGE AND MATURITY ASSIST IN ATTAINING SHALOM BAYIS

A woman who was having severe *Shalom Bayis* problems, inquired of the Rebbe whether to try to keep the family together, or whether to try to build a new life.

The Rebbe responded that the person should try to keep the family together. The Rebbe also added the following:

(1) From time to time to make an effort to better the situation, doing so again and again — with the assistance of a psychologist and medication.

Most importantly, your husband desires this as well, [i.e., that the marriage last,] for it is to his benefit (even in his view) and the benefit of the children *sheyichyu*.

The more your husband matures, the more there is weakened within him the intensity of "the days of youth and their fervor," and his rationality dominates to a greater extent (what is truly best for *him* in all the above).

Thus, after *many, many* years of finding yourself in such a situation, surely the misery of the situation has lessened and is not as great as it was in the beginning.

(2) That would mean [i.e., a divorce would mean,] to destroy, G-d forbid, all that presently exists and to begin *searching* anew a new manner of life for yourself and your children (accompanied by the never-ending doubt as to whether you did the correct thing by destroying [the marriage], or whether you lost the chance [to rectify the situation]).

(3) Our Sages declare that "Great is peace," and that "the Divine Presence resides in their midst," etc. Understandably, then, you should make the effort [to attain *Shalom Bayis*].

I will mention you in prayer at the holy resting site of my father-in-law, the Rebbe.

(*Nitzutzei Or*, p. 9)

THE REBBE'S AVOIDANCE OF OFFERING HIS CONSENT TO A DIVORCE

... As to the request in your letter that I write clearly [about the advisability of a divorce]:

There is the known directive concerning conduct in such matters, and so too have I actually witnessed the conduct of my father-in-law, the Rebbe, that he would avoid saying "no" [even] with regard to negating a *shidduch*. And most definitely would he avoid giving his imprimatur on a matter of "separation," [i.e., a divorce].

This is particularly so — and as I have already written to your son — since by the time the letters go back and forth matters can change with regard to many particulars. Therefore, your son should seek your counsel as well as the counsel of his friends from our community who are already aware of the situation.

May G-d grant those who counsel your son the proper insight so that they make the appropriate decision.

I await glad tidings with regard to all the above.

(*Igros Kodesh*, Vol. VIII, p. 176)

The Rebbe's Extreme Avoidance of Pressuring for the Issuance of a Divorce

It is not at all customary that I should pressure for ... a divorce! The reason for this is readily understandable.

In general, this matter belongs to a *Rav*.

(From a handwritten response of the Rebbe)[8]

Our Sages Have Absolutely Negated Divorce

Our Sages, of blessed memory, have spoken in the most glowing terms with regard to *Shalom Bayis*, and have absolutely negated the matter of a divorce, G-d forbid.

In your situation [in particular]: G-d has blessed you with children who surely need a [proper] home, etc., [i.e., a home that has both a father and mother]. Therefore you should continue [your marriage] and be the *Akeres HaBayis*, the "foundation and mainstay of the home," and may G-d crown your efforts with success.

Understandably —as is the Jewish custom — you and your husband can together set forth your situation before a *Rav* and ask him to mediate, etc.

(From a written response of the Rebbe, from the year 5730)

8. Printed in *Kfar Chabad* Magazine (together with a facsimile of the Rebbe's holy handwritten response), Issue 878.